FROM CHAOS TO CONFIDENCE:

A BUSY MOM'S GUIDE TO PARENTING WITH HEART AND SKILL

STEPHANIE ULFIG

ISBN: 978-1-963977-31-8

Published in the United States of America by Greenlamp Publishing, an imprint of Greenlamp LLC, Orange County, California.

Greenlamp Publishing
30021 Tomas, Suite 300
Rancho Santa Margarita, CA 92688

DEDICATION

To every busy mother who juggles endless demands with boundless love—this book is for you. May these words offer a gentle embrace, guiding you through the chaos and reminding you that your strength, resilience, and compassion illuminate the path for your family. You are seen, you are valued, and you have the power to create the support you need.

TABLE OF CONTENTS

ACKNOWLEDGEMENTS

I am deeply grateful for the gift of research and the critical knowledge it provides—knowledge that empowers us to raise resilient, thriving children. I extend my heartfelt thanks to the many researchers, mentors, teachers, and fellow mothers whose insights and experiences have enriched these pages. Your commitment to learning and growth inspires mothers everywhere to nurture strength, resilience, and joy in every child.

NOTE FROM THE AUTHOR

Motherhood is one of the most profound and transformative journeys a woman can embark upon. It is filled with moments of overwhelming joy, deep love, and, at times, fear and uncertainty. I know this because I have lived it.

When I became a mother, I quickly realized that while love for my children came naturally, the skills and confidence to navigate motherhood was something I had to develop over time.

I had visions of joy-filled days and a deep, unshakable connection with my children. But what I wasn't prepared for were the moments of exhaustion, self-doubt, and guilt. I felt lost—questioning whether I was doing enough, whether I was getting it right, whether I was the mother my children truly needed. I carried the weight of my mistakes, the pain of my shortcomings, and the fear that I wasn't enough.

And yet, through all of it, I tried my best. Even on the hardest days, I showed up. I learned, I grew, and I kept going because my love for my children was stronger than my fears. Over time, I realized that motherhood is not about perfection—it's about perseverance in the face of challenges, self-awareness to recognize where I can grow, the courage to repair my mistakes, and a willingness to learn every step of the way.

This book was born from my journey, my education and my work with parents. I wrote it for every mother who has ever felt overwhelmed, uncertain, or simply in need of guidance and support. Within these pages, you'll find some of the core foundational elements of parenting, not as rigid rules, but as tools to help you create a nurturing, loving, and thriving environment for your child.

Parenting is not a one-size-fits-all journey, but by embracing key principles and trusting yourself, you can create an environment where both you and your child thrive. You are already an incredible mother simply because you care deeply. I hope this book helps you see that, and that it gives you the confidence to embrace your journey.

With love and support,

Stephanie

PREFACE

WHY IS IT NECESSARY TO START WITH INNER WORK?

In the journey of motherhood, the most transformative work begins within. Inner work is the foundation that empowers you to nurture not only your own well-being but also the well-being of your children. When you invest in self-awareness, self-compassion, and healing, you break old patterns and build resilience, enabling you to navigate the complexities of parenting with clarity and confidence. This preface explores "why" starting with inner work is essential for every mother who aspires to create a home filled with love, balance, and genuine connection.

If you're seeking a quick fix, slow down and work on your inner self first.

In a world full of parenting hacks, expert advice, and quick-fix solutions, it is tempting to look for the fastest way to solve parenting challenges; however, the key to long-term success isn't in external strategies—it starts within. Slowing down and developing self-awareness, emotional regulation, and inner confidence leads to more effective, lasting change in parenting.

Here are six reasons why:

1. Parenting Strategies Work Best When Applied from a Grounded Place

Mothers often search for external solutions, not realizing that their emotional state plays a crucial role in how effective any solution can work. Even the most effective parenting techniques are likely to backfire, leaving you exhausted, if they're applied from a place of stress, fear, or self-doubt. Children are highly attuned to their mother's energy, responding more to how she feels than what she says or does. When a mother is overwhelmed or uncertain, her child may react with resistance or insecurity. But when she approaches parenting with confidence, calm, and emotional clarity, even simple strategies become more effective and nurturing.

Take the mother who is struggling with her child's bedtime routine. Most of us have experienced this. We might search for the best sleep-training method, trying different techniques like setting timers, offering rewards, or using a firm approach. However, if you're feeling anxious and doubtful—worrying about whether you're handling the situation right or fearing your child will never sleep well— your child will sense that uncertainty. This can lead to increased bedtime resistance, more crying, or clinginess, ultimately making the process even more challenging.

On the other hand, you can be the mother who takes time to regulate your emotions and approaches bedtime with confidence and calm, which helps your child feel more secure. Instead of focusing solely on external solutions, you remind yourself that consistency, patience, and emotional reassurance matter most. By calmly saying, "It's time for bed now. I love you, and I'll see you in the morning," with a steady tone and reassuring presence, your child is more likely to settle down. Never lose sight of the fact that your emotional clarity makes even a simple bedtime routine more effective and nurturing.

2. Quick Fixes Don't Address the Root of the Problem

Surface-level solutions may offer temporary relief, but if a mother's stress, past experiences, or limiting beliefs go unchecked, the same challenges will keep resurfacing. True, lasting change in parenting comes from within—by addressing unresolved emotions, shifting negative thought patterns, and developing self-awareness. So, when mothers take the time to heal, grow, and manage their own well-being, she not only finds more effective solutions but also creates a healthier, more nurturing environment for her child.

For example, a mother who struggles with her child's defiant behavior. Does this sound familiar? Most moms experience this at some point in their child's development. You may try various discipline techniques—timeouts, reward charts, or stricter rules—to regain control. While some of these strategies might work temporarily, the pattern doesn't break, and you find yourself repeatedly facing the same power struggles.

By looking deeper, you might realize that frustration stems from your own childhood experiences of feeling unheard or powerless. This is why your child's defiance triggers old wounds in you, causing you to react with either excessive control or emotional overwhelm.

Take time to reflect, heal, and shift your mindset in these situations—perhaps through journaling, therapy, or self-compassion—you can start to respond differently, which takes away the negative energy and replaces it with practical solutions. Instead of viewing your child's defiance as a personal challenge, you've reframed it as an opportunity to guide them with patience and connection. This inner growth will help you approach discipline more effectively, while also nurturing a more secure and trusting relationship with your child, creating lasting change rather than temporary fixes.

3. Children Mirror Their Mother's Emotional State

Kids don't just listen to what their mothers say—they absorb how they feel. Children are incredibly perceptive, picking up on their mother's emotions, energy, and unspoken cues. When a mother is calm and confident, her child feels secure. when she is anxious or overwhelmed, her child senses it, often mirroring those emotions. more than words, a mother's presence, tone, and emotional state shape how her child experiences the world and responds to it.

Consider the mother who feels anxious about her child starting pre-school. She repeatedly reassures them, saying, "You'll be fine! It's going to be so much fun!" But who is she really reassuring, the child or their self. If her tone is tense, her body language stiff, and her face filled with worry, her child will pick up on that anxiety. Instead of feeling excited and secure, they may become hesitant, clingy, or fearful, mirroring their mother's unease. Has this every been you?

On the other hand, you can be the mother who takes time to regulate your emotions. It's great to acknowledge your worries but the approach you take with your children should be one of calm confidence. And one thing about little kids is you cannot fool them with your energy, they are at a natural state of intuitiveness. If you warmly say, "I know new things can feel a little scary at first, but I trust you'll have a great time," while maintaining a steady tone and relaxed posture, her child is more likely to feel safe and approach the transition with confidence. Your emotional state, more than your words, sets the tone for how your child experiences the moment.

4. Self-Awareness Helps Mothers Parent from Intention, Not Fear

When anxiety drives parenting decisions, it often leads to over-control, inconsistency, or guilt-driven choices—reacting out of fear rather than intention. This can create a cycle where a mother second-guesses herself, struggles to set boundaries, or tries to fix every problem immediately. Slowing down creates space for clarity, allowing mothers to respond with patience and wisdom rather than react impulsively. When you parent from your values instead of your fears, you cultivate trust, stability, and a deeper connection with your children.

For example, If you're a mother who feels anxious about your child's struggles in school, your initial reaction might be to micromanage their homework, constantly correct mistakes, or push them to perform better. However, this over-controlling approach—driven by fear—can trigger power struggles, resistance, and ultimately undermine your child's self-confidence. And as a loving mother, that's the last thing you want to see.

However, if you choose to slow down and reflect on your core values—perhaps growth, resilience, and emotional well-being—you might approach the situation differently. Instead of reacting with control, you could offer support by helping your child to develop problem-solving skills, creating a calm study environment, and encouraging effort over perfection. By parenting from values over fears, you have an incredible opportunity to foster confidence and independence in your child rather than stress and pressure.

5. Inner Work Reduces Burnout and Overwhelm

When a mother focuses only on fixing external problems—managing her child's behavior, keeping up with daily demands, or seeking the perfect parenting strategy—without addressing her own emotional well-being, she quickly becomes exhausted and resentful. The constant effort to control everything outside herself drains her energy and leaves her feeling unappreciated or overwhelmed. However, when she takes the time to understand and regulate her own emotions—whether through self-reflection, mindfulness, or self-care—she gains a greater sense of control from within. Instead of reacting out of stress or frustration, she can respond with patience, clarity, and confidence, creating a more balanced and fulfilling parenting experience.

Are you a mother overwhelmed by your child's relentless tantrums? It's an incredibly frustrating experience. You may have turned to parenting books, stricter rules, or various discipline techniques in an effort to, solve the issue. Yet, these strategies rarely yield lasting results if you're operating from a place of frustration and exhaustion. In fact, this approach can increase your risk of feeling resentful toward your child—only deepening the cycle of negative emotions and leaving you feeling even worse.

If you take time to check in with yourself—recognizing triggers, managing stress, and practicing self-regulation—you gain the emotional resilience to handle the situation more effectively. Instead of reacting with anger or frustration, you can stay calm during a tantrum, validate your child's emotions, and set boundaries with patience. By prioritizing your own emotional well-being, you not only feel more in control but also model emotional regulation for your child, leading to a healthier dynamic for both of you.

6. Long-Term Change Comes from the Inside Out

Slowing down doesn't mean doing less—it means approaching parenting with greater intention and clarity. When mothers pause to cultivate self-awareness, emotional intelligence, and inner security, they make choices that align with their values rather than reacting out of stress or fear. This shift invites more presence, patience, and responsiveness to a child's needs. Instead of constantly searching for the next parenting strategy or feeling pressured to "do more," the key is to trust yourself more, navigate challenges with confidence, and create a more peaceful, fulfilling experience for everyone.

If you feel overwhelmed by your child's constant whining, you might instinctively try to fix the behavior by offering rewards, setting stricter rules, or searching for the perfect discipline technique. However, if you do these steps out of frustration laced with a bit of self-doubt, you will be inconsistent. Sometimes you'll give in and other times you'll just snap in irritation, which leads to even more whining.

By slowing down and being self-aware and emotionally regulated, you can recognize that your frustration comes from feeling unheard or overstretched. Instead of immediately reacting, it's okay to take a deep breath, center yourself, and respond in a calmer, more confident way. Your child can have their feelings validated and you can maintain firm, clear boundaries at the same time. It starts with a shift of mindset that guides you from fixing the behavior to understanding the emotions and situation. All this starts with inner confidence that is not reliant on endless external solutions.

Final Reflection

By slowing down and working on your inner self first, you can nurture the confidence, emotional stability, and self-awareness that form the foundation of effective parenting. This is a situation where the search for external fixes cannot supersede the internal work of learning to trust yourself, respond rather than react, and create a home environment rooted in security and connection.

Additionally, this inner work not only helps you to navigate challenges with greater ease while setting a powerful example for your children. You have a tremendous opportunity to teach your little one's resilience, emotional intelligence, and self-trust. It all begins with prioritizing your own growth and well-being so you can blaze forward with an example for your children that leads to meaningful changes that benefit both of you, and that is the ultimate act of self-love and love for your child.

Book Purpose

My purpose in writing this book is to empower mothers to become intentional, confident, and emotionally attuned parents by helping them understand the transformative role self-awareness plays in parenting.

I want to introduce growth-focused mothers to the journey of self-discovery—one that allows you to break free from harmful patterns, embrace personal growth, and show up for your children with clarity and confidence.

Parenting isn't just about managing a child's behavior; it's about understanding ourselves—our triggers, emotions, and past experiences—so we can respond with wisdom rather than react from stress or fear. When we commit to our own growth, we create a more nurturing, stable environment where both we and our children can thrive.

This book is about transformation. My hope is that through these pages, you will discover the power of self-awareness, begin to develop the emotional resilience needed for the challenges of motherhood, and ultimately, cultivate a deeper, more fulfilling connection with your child.

How to use this book

This book is designed to be a practical and approachable guide, offering simple yet powerful strategies that you can easily integrate into your daily life. Key concepts are intentionally reinforced throughout to deepen understanding and support lasting growth, making it easier to apply these insights in real-life parenting situations.

The exercises are concise and manageable, helping you take small, meaningful steps without feeling overwhelmed. By engaging with these strategies consistently, you will strengthen self-awareness, parent with confidence, and nurture deeper, healthier connections with your children.

INTRODUCTION

THE JOURNEY TO SELF-AWARE MOTHERHOOD

Parents do more than simply raise children—they embark on a transformative journey alongside them. Parenthood isn't just about guiding a child's growth; it's an evolution of self. When a child is born, a parent experiences a kind of rebirth, stepping into a role that reshapes their identity, challenges their perspectives, and invites continuous learning. This journey can feel exhilarating yet disorienting, like navigating an ever-turning carousel. But here's the truth: you're not just along for the ride. You have the power to find your balance, embrace growth, and steer with intention. The choice is yours.

Nobody truly prepares us for this moment. Advice from friends may not quite fit your reality, and no matter how many social media parenting tips you consume, they remain broad, impersonal snapshots—not tailored to you or your child. I once read that *"motherhood is an opportunity to work on your own shadow."* That idea stayed with me. It's both profound and empowering—a reminder that in raising our children, we are also confronting and refining ourselves. Motherhood is not just about nurturing a child; it's a journey of self-discovery,

1

growth, and the deep, transformative bond that shapes both mother and child along the way.

Can you relate to this journey? If you're still in the thick of it—navigating the highs and lows of motherhood—this book is for you, no matter how old your child(ren) may be. Inside, you'll find practical, actionable tools designed to help you cultivate an intentional and emotionally healthy approach to motherhood—one that aligns with your unique experiences, not anyone else's expectations.

It all begins with self-awareness. By becoming attuned to your emotions, thoughts, and behavioral patterns, you'll uncover parts of yourself that have long been buried—waiting for motherhood's challenges to bring them to the surface. This is a turning point, not a time to give up. I can tell you from experience: doing the inner work transforms parenthood in ways you never imagined. It won't suddenly make motherhood effortless—let's be real—but it will equip you with the clarity and resilience to navigate challenges, embrace the joys, and show up as the mother you truly want to be.

The power of this book lies in its practicality—it's easy to digest, designed for your (very limited, we know) spare moments, and built to fit seamlessly into your busy life. Self-awareness isn't just a tool; it's a game-changer, saving you time, disappointment, and frustration. But more importantly, it challenges the belief that *"This is just who I am."* No—you are not only capable of more, but you *want* more. Growth is always possible. Change is always within reach.

This journey begins with a deep exploration of self-awareness in motherhood—what it truly means and why it matters. Self-awareness is the foundation of intentional parenting, where you consciously prioritize your time and energy to model healthy behaviors and fully engage with your child. Parenthood inevitably comes with anxiety, burnout, and stress, but these challenges deserve your attention, not just as burdens to bear, but as obstacles that can be understood and overcome. By addressing them with intention, you pave the way for a more present, connected, and fulfilling parenting experience.

None of us step into motherhood as a blank slate. Our upbringing—whether nurturing or challenging—shapes our parenting in ways we may not even realize, embedding subconscious beliefs that influence our choices. Becoming aware of these patterns is the key to breaking free from unhelpful habits and parenting with intention. This isn't about blaming the past or assuming our childhood was inherently flawed. Rather, it's about recognizing that many of our actions, behaviors, and beliefs are shaped by history rather than aligned with our true values. Along the journey of motherhood, it's easy to lose sight of what truly matters to us. But with awareness, we can reclaim it.

It's time to embrace the support that's already here for you and uncover what truly matters—beyond the expectations of family, friends, or society. This is your opportunity to reconnect with yourself and step into a new chapter—one where you show up as the best version of yourself, not just for your children, but for you. Because the most meaningful care you can give isn't rooted in external pressures—it comes from within, from a mother's heart that is present, self-aware, and deeply aligned with what matters most.

This transformation begins by turning inward and identifying what beliefs, patterns, and reactions are not truly yours. If you're thinking, *Easier said than done*, you're not alone—I've been there too. But I can tell you from experience that awareness is the first and most powerful step. I never wanted to repeat the unempathetic or intimidating behaviors I experienced as a child, yet without realizing it, I found myself echoing them. Breaking that cycle required me to see those patterns clearly, release them, and make space for something more intentional, more compassionate—something truly my own.

Moms, if there's one thing parenting reveals, it's the emotional triggers that lurk beneath the surface. These triggers can feel like the enemy, hijacking your reactions and making you question yourself. But the truth is, they aren't working against you—they're revealing wounds that need attention. The hardest part? Many of these wounds have been buried for years. Confronting them isn't easy, but consider this: facing them means breaking the cycle, ensuring that your children don't carry the same burdens. When we look at it that way, the challenge becomes an opportunity—one that's worth every ounce of effort.

Once we grasp the foundation of these ideas, the real transformation begins. This is where the exercises and tools come in—practical strategies to cultivate self-awareness, break free from negative patterns, and align our actions with what truly matters. No more reacting on autopilot, driven by past wounds, subconscious beliefs, or emotional triggers. Instead, we step into conscious, intentional motherhood, guided by our higher self.

Will this book solve everything? Of course not. I'd never make such a promise because, frankly, that concept doesn't exist! And that's okay. The most profound growth comes from the challenges we face with courage, and this journey will be one of them.

From this point forward, you have a choice: continue down the familiar road, repeating patterns that no longer serve you, or take the path of inner work—a road that may be more challenging but leads to breakthroughs beyond what you can imagine. I won't spoil the discovery for you because this is something you have to experience for yourself. And when you do, you'll see just how powerful and capable you truly are.

PART 1

UNDERSTANDING SELF-AWARENESS IN MOTHERHOOD

CHAPTER 1

WHAT IS SELF-AWARENESS AND
WHY DOES IT MATTER?

Moms are constantly in motion—juggling responsibilities, meeting endless demands, and showing up for everyone around them. In the midst of it all, it's easy to forget that we are human too. How often do we truly pause and check in with ourselves? And what does that even look like?

The pauses we take aren't just moments of rest—they are opportunities to reconnect with our thoughts, emotions, and actions. So much of our daily life runs on autopilot, shaped by patterns we may not even realize we're following. But when we choose to slow down and examine our reactions, we gain the power to change them for the better.

Here's what every parent should know: self-awareness is the foundation of intentional parenting. It allows us to make conscious choices, free from emotional triggers, childhood wounds, and subconscious beliefs. And self-awareness is more than simply recognizing our feelings—it's about seeing ourselves with clarity, objectivity, and compassion. Research shows that when we cultivate this awareness, our confidence grows, our creativity flourishes, and our ability to make thoughtful decisions strengthens. The result? We foster deeper connections, communicate more effectively, and create lasting, meaningful relationships.

People who take shortcuts or remain in their comfort zones often do so because they haven't developed self-awareness. After all, it's not exactly *fun* to take a hard look at ourselves—especially when we're facing something uncomfortable. *Why was I so quick to anger? Why is it so hard to get through to my kids?* These are just two of the many self-critiquing questions that can arise in the heat of parenting. But what we often forget is that we are not meant to be perfect. Growth begins with recognizing what isn't working—an ego check, for sure, but an essential step toward becoming the parents we aspire to be.

When we stop avoiding our inner worlds, we gain the ability to see ourselves more clearly—not just our struggles, but also our values, passions, and aspirations. We begin to understand how to align these truths with the realities of our lives: our unique parenting circumstances, our children's personalities, our time constraints, and so much more. This shift allows us to recognize why we parent the way we do, deepen our connection with our children, and make intentional choices that reflect our most authentic values.

Intentional parenting has become a beacon of hope for mothers, offering a path toward deeper connection and greater fulfillment in their parenting journey. Its growing popularity is no coincidence—it's an approach rooted in mindfulness and purpose, benefiting not only children but also parents themselves. Yes, *all* parents can benefit from this! While cultivating deliberate actions and mindful responses isn't always easy, shifting away from knee-jerk emotional reactions allows us to step into the role of the parents we *aspire* to be—the ones our children truly need.

One of the greatest gifts of self-awareness is the ability to be *fully present*. The fact that you are here, exploring this work, shows just how much you care about your motherhood journey. This inner work doesn't just transform *you*—it helps you see your children more clearly, recognize their unique personalities, and parent in a way that honors who they are. It equips you to set healthy boundaries, prioritize meaningful connection, and cultivate a parenting approach that is both intentional and deeply fulfilling.

Our words, actions, and decisions leave a lasting imprint on our children—whether we realize it or not. Just as the words and behaviors of our own parents shaped us, our interactions with our children will shape their hearts and minds. Wouldn't it be empowering to approach parenting with greater intention, making conscious choices that align with the values we want to instill?

But let's be honest—this is no easy task. Parenting is demanding, and I say this with complete sincerity. The stress, anxiety, and sheer exhaustion that come with raising children can keep us in a relentless cycle of survival. A single unanticipated trigger can push us over the edge. Sleepless nights erode our patience and clarity. The deep-seated fear of something happening to our children makes us react impulsively, in ways we might not in other situations. It's not that we don't want to parent with intention—it's that the weight of it all can make it feel impossible.

Emotional Regulation, Decision-Making, and Connection with Our Kids

Children learn more from what we do than from what we say. They watch us closely, absorbing how we manage our emotions and handle challenges. This is why practicing emotional regulation and intentional decision-making is so crucial—it allows us to show up fully present in our interactions with them.

When stress, anxiety, and burnout take over, however, we slip into survival mode, reacting impulsively rather than modeling a healthy, grounded way of being. Ask yourself: Do I know how to regulate my emotions? Can I make clear, intentional decisions? Am I truly present in the moment? If you're unsure, know that these struggles can make it harder to meet your child's needs with patience and attunement.

On the other hand, when parents are emotionally regulated, they create a safe and stable environment—one that directly influences their child's attachment style and their ability to navigate vulnerability. Beyond that, emotionally regulated individuals make more thoughtful, conscious choices. By developing this skill ourselves, we equip our children with the foundation to make confident, self-assured decisions throughout their lives.

At the heart of effective parenting lies the art of emotional regulation. But what does that truly mean? It's our capacity to recognize our emotions and manage them in a way that nurtures a balanced response, rather than allowing ourselves to be swept away by overwhelming feelings.

Emotional regulation isn't about suppressing or denying what we feel. It's about understanding our inner landscape—acknowledging each emotion, making room for it, and then choosing a thoughtful, measured response. When we learn these skills, our emotions become allies rather than adversaries, guiding us to respond with clarity and compassion.

Suppressing our emotions is like trying to fill a bottomless pit—it never leads us to a fulfilling place. Instead, by recognizing and embracing our feelings, we give ourselves the space to pause, reflect, and expand our range of responses. In doing so, we empower our parenting journey, allowing our values and aspirations to shape our decisions rather than being dictated by raw, unchecked emotion.

This process isn't about eliminating feelings—it's about reclaiming control. With emotional regulation, we build a resilient foundation that helps us navigate the unpredictable world of motherhood, fostering both our well-being and the nurturing environment our children deserve.

Parenthood is a journey of endless choices—a tapestry of decisions woven through each day that can sometimes feel overwhelmingly chaotic. In moments like these, you might even feel as fragile as a broken egg, scattered by the rush of emotions. Yet, every decision you make carries the weight of nurturing another human being, a responsibility that is both daunting and deeply profound.

When we cultivate self-awareness and learn to regulate our emotions, we transform this whirlwind into a space of clarity. By gently pausing to observe our feelings, we empower ourselves to evaluate various options without becoming overwhelmed. This measured approach not only illuminates the most thoughtful course of action but also opens our eyes to creative solutions that might otherwise remain hidden.

In embracing emotional regulation, we discover that our responses become guided by reason and compassion. This clarity doesn't diminish the intensity of our love or the depth of our care—it simply allows us to navigate the challenges of motherhood with greater resilience and wisdom. Ultimately, when our inner balance is restored, the path of parenthood becomes a smoother, more intentional journey where both our hearts and minds are in harmonious dialogue.

Reflection Exercise: Self-Awareness Scorecard

This self-awareness scorecard will help you assess how present, intentional, and emotionally aware you are in your parenting. This exercise is not meant as a way to judge yourself. It is a tool to identify your strengths and those areas that need some adjustments, in order to continue growing and become the parent you want to be.

Step 1: Assess Your Starting Point

On a scale of 1 to 5 *(1 = Rarely, 5 = Almost Always)*, rate yourself on the following statements:

Emotional Awareness

_____ I recognize my emotions before reacting to my child's behavior.

_____ I can identify when I'm feeling overwhelmed and take steps to regulate myself.

_____ I notice patterns in my moods and how they affect my parenting.

Intentional Parenting

_____ I pause and think before responding to my child's challenging behaviors.

_____ I parent based on my values, not just habits or reactions.

_____ I reflect on what is working and what isn't in my parenting approach.

Handling Triggers & Stress

_____ I am aware of specific parenting situations that trigger frustration or anxiety in me.

_____ I take responsibility for my emotional reactions rather than blaming my child.

_____ I use strategies like deep breathing or stepping away when I need to calm down.

Growth Mindset & Adaptability

_____ I allow myself to make mistakes and model learning from them for my child.

_____ I actively seek ways to improve my parenting rather than feeling stuck in old habits.

_____ I remind myself that self-awareness is an ongoing journey, not a destination.

Step 2: Reflect on Your Results

Which areas did you score the highest? → These are your strengths, keep nurturing them!

Write a short letter congratulating yourself for having these strengths. Do it in the most authentic way possible.

_____

_____

_____

_____

_____

Which areas scored the lowest? → These show opportunities for growth, not failure.

Connect with your most compassionate side and let it express itself in the following lines. What words of support would it give you? What small changes can you make this week to improve these areas?

_____

_____

_____

_____

_____

Step 3: Set an Intention for Growth

Choose one area where you'd like to improve your self-awareness. Example: *"I want to work on recognizing my emotions before reacting to my child's behavior."*

_____

_____

_____

_____

_____

_____

Now, write one small, actionable step you can take this week to grow in this area. Example: *"I will pause and take three deep breaths before responding when I feel frustrated."*

_____

_____

_____

_____

_____

_____

Final Reflection

Self-awareness is a muscle: it gets stronger with practice! Revisit this scorecard in a few weeks and notice how you have grown.

CHAPTER 2

RECOGNIZING YOUR PARENTING BLUEPRINT

Human babies are uniquely helpless compared to many other primates and are born in a state of complete vulnerability, utterly dependent on a caregiver for survival. From the very first moment of life, we rely on the presence, care, and responsiveness of others to thrive.

But who those caregivers are—and the experiences they bring with them—varies greatly. Each parent steps into the role with their own beliefs, values, parenting styles, emotional wounds, and personal history. Layered onto this is the influence of social, cultural, and historical contexts. Our parents raised us within a different world—one shaped by the expectations, tools, and norms of their time, many of which may feel distant or even incompatible with today's parenting landscape.

Whether we align with their approach or resist it entirely, our upbringing leaves an undeniable imprint on us. And when we become parents ourselves, these deep-seated influences inevitably rise to the surface. Remember what we discussed about modeling in the previous chapter? We learn, first and foremost, by observing. The way our parents disciplined us, spoke to us, reassured us, and set boundaries subtly informs the strategies we use with our own children—often without us even realizing it.

Some of us unconsciously repeat the patterns we experienced as children, while others, determined to break away, swing to the opposite extreme. But true growth as a parent comes not from blindly following or rejecting the past, but from consciously choosing what aligns with our values, what nurtures connection, and what allows us to show up as the kind of parents we aspire to be.

Research shows that the experiences of our own childhood craft the very blueprint of our emotional responses and the ways we navigate our feelings as adults. When we step into the role of a parent, our children, completely reliant on us for survival, naturally ignite our deepest emotional currents. In these moments, the generational patterns that have been silently woven through our family histories often emerge with unexpected force.

Every family carries its own legacy—a pattern of behavior passed down through the years, evolving subtly with each generation. Often, we find ourselves unconsciously echoing the parenting styles we once knew, whether they were nurturing or flawed. It's in those challenging moments, when you catch yourself acting out of habit rather than intention, that the "why" behind your parenting blueprint becomes clear.

These patterns—formed from long-held beliefs, values, and dynamics—can sometimes feel elusive, even impossible to dismantle, especially when they harbor unhealthy elements. Yet, acknowledging these inherited influences is the first courageous step toward redefining the narrative for your family. By understanding and addressing these patterns, you open the door to more conscious, compassionate parenting that honors both your past and the future you wish to create.

Many of us accept the behaviors and beliefs passed down through generations as simply "the way things are"—the unspoken rules that keep our family dynamic predictably intact, even if they aren't always healthy. When these patterns go unquestioned, they become the norm, sometimes even turning into taboos, making it nearly impossible to imagine a different way of being.

Our unique upbringings shape our parenting in profound ways. For instance, those raised under strict, authoritarian rules may feel compelled to demand obedience and exert control over their children. On the other hand, a highly permissive upbringing can leave us struggling to set necessary boundaries.

Now, imagine a parenting approach that centers on open communication and emotional support—a nurture-based model that places your child's psychological well-being at its core. In this paradigm, you become attuned to your child's inner world, cultivating an environment where feelings are understood and respected. By embracing this mindful method, you not only honor your child's emotional needs but also break free from inherited patterns, creating a more conscious, compassionate family legacy.

I truly believe that each new generation holds the promise to nurture healthier parenting and heal the wounds of the past. We have the opportunity to offer our children what we might have missed, laying the foundation for them to, in turn, create a more loving legacy for their own children.

With that vision in mind, I've come to accept that the notion of being the "perfect mother" is not only unattainable but also an unhealthy ideal to chase. Embracing this truth means making peace with imperfection and releasing the intense pressure we often place on ourselves—and sometimes on others. The relentless pursuit of perfection can turn us into pressure cookers on the verge of explosion, which only fuels reactivity and impulsivity, perpetuating those unconscious patterns we long to break.

Instead, by dedicating ourselves to being the best parent we can be, we become more than "good enough" for our children. This mindset, centered on growth and compassion, transforms our journey into one of mindful parenting—one that nurtures both our well-being and that of our family.

Self-awareness is the most powerful tool we have to break free from the cultural influences and generational patterns that have shaped our upbringing. By reflecting on our childhood experiences, we can begin to understand how they influence our reactions and decisions as parents. This honest self-examination is the essential first step towards making conscious, intentional choices that resonate with our deepest values.

It's important to remember that not every aspect of our past is a flaw to be discarded. Instead, we have the opportunity to thoughtfully select which parts of our upbringing we wish to honor and incorporate into our own parenting style—and which parts we consciously choose to leave behind or transform. By engaging in this reflective practice, we free ourselves from the autopilot mode that can so easily govern our actions. In doing so, we gradually cultivate the kind of parenting that truly reflects who we are and who we aspire to be.

Exercise: Family Influence Mapping

As we've discussed before, our parenting styles are profoundly shaped by the way we were raised. Often, we remain unaware of how our core beliefs, emotional patterns, and habitual reactions are rooted in our childhood experiences, societal expectations, and the legacy of generational influences.

This exercise is designed to guide you on a reflective journey that will illuminate the unconscious family patterns influencing your parenting style. Through thoughtful self-observation, you'll identify which influences you wish to honor, which to adapt, and which to let go of, empowering you to parent with greater intentionality and self-awareness.

Step 1: Create a Calm Space

- **Find Your Sanctuary:** Choose a quiet time and place where you feel safe and undisturbed—this might be a cozy corner of your home, a favorite park bench, or simply a time when you can be alone with your thoughts.
- **Gather Your Tools:** Have a journal or notepad, a pen, and optionally, some calming music or a cup of tea to set a relaxed tone.

Step 2: Reflect on Your Childhood

- **Memory Mapping:** Begin by writing down vivid memories from your childhood—moments that stand out, whether they evoked comfort or discomfort. Don't worry about organizing them perfectly; let the memories flow freely.
- **Identify Themes:** Look for recurring themes or patterns in these memories. What values, behaviors, or emotional responses seem to have been a constant presence in your family?

Your Experience as a Child

How did your parents or caregivers express love and affection?

_____

_____

_____

_____

_____

What were the discipline methods used in your home?

_____

_____

_____

_____

_____

Were emotions openly discussed in your family, or were they avoided?

_____

_____

_____

_____

_____

How did your parents handle stress, conflict, or disappointment?

_____

_____

_____

_____

_____

Did you feel heard and validated as a child? Why or why not?

_____

_____

_____

_____

_____

Were there any specific phrases or messages about parenting that stuck with you? Example: *"Children should be seen, not heard." "Stop crying, it's not a big deal." "Be strong, don't be weak."*

_____

_____

_____

_____

_____

The Emotional Blueprint You Inherited

What emotions were safe to express in your childhood home? Which emotions were discouraged?

_____

_____

_____

_____

Did your parent's model healthy emotional regulation, or did they struggle with managing their emotions?

_____

_____

_____

_____

_____

What role did gender play in emotional expression? *(Example: Were boys encouraged to be tough, and girls encouraged to be nurturing?)*

_____

_____

_____

_____

_____

How did your family handle mistakes and failure? Were they met with shame, punishment, or growth opportunities?

_____

_____

_____

_____

_____

Messages About Self-Worth and Success

What was your family's definition of a "good child"?

_____

_____

_____

_____

_____

Did you feel pressure to be perfect, achieve high standards, or meet specific expectations?

_____

_____

_____

_____

_____

How did your parents or caregivers talk about self-care, boundaries, or taking breaks? Example: *"Rest is lazy." "Mothers must sacrifice everything for their children."*

_____

_____

_____

_____

_____

Step 3: Recognize What You've Carried into Parenthood

Now that you've explored how you were raised let's connect it to your current parenting patterns.

Which of these beliefs or behaviors do you find yourself repeating in your parenting?

Do you use a similar discipline style to your parents?

_____

_____

_____

_____

_____

Do you react to stress the way your parents did?

_____

_____

_____

_____

_____

Are there certain emotions you struggle to validate in your child because they were not validated in you?

_____

_____

_____

_____

_____

Which beliefs or patterns do you want to break?
What parenting messages or behaviors from your childhood **don't** align with your values today?

_____

_____

_____

_____

_____

Are there any generational patterns (such as emotional suppression, fear-based discipline, or lack of boundaries) that you want to change?

_____

_____

_____

_____

_____

In what ways do you desire to respond differently to challenges than your parents did?

_____

_____

_____

_____

_____

What strengths did your parents model that you want to keep?
Did they demonstrate resilience, kindness, or patience?

_____

_____

_____

_____

_____

Were there traditions or practices that brought security and connection?

_____

_____

_____

_____

_____

What lessons from your upbringing have positively shaped the way you parent?

_____

_____

_____

_____

_____

Step 4: Categorize the Influences

Divide your observations into three categories:

1. **Honor:** List the beliefs, behaviors, or emotional responses that provided a positive influence on you. These are the qualities you want to carry forward into your parenting.
   Journal Prompt: "What lessons from my past fill me with gratitude and strength? How have these positive influences shaped who I am today?"

2. **Adapt:** Identify those aspects that, while meaningful, might need a fresh perspective or slight adjustment to better serve you and your children.
   Journal Prompt: "Which inherited behaviors could be modified

to better align with my current values? What new practices could honor the past while meeting the needs of today?"

3. **Release:** Recognize the patterns or beliefs that no longer serve you—or that have caused pain—and that you feel ready to let go of.

Create a Diagram: On a blank page, draw three columns labeled "Honor," "Adapt," and "Release." Place each identified influence under its respective heading. Visualizing these patterns can help clarify their role in your life and highlight areas for intentional change.

Rewrite Your Parenting Narrative

Now that you've identified the influences shaping your parenting let's take intentional steps toward change.

Journal Prompts for Rewriting Your Parenting Narrative:

If I could describe the kind of parent I want to be in one sentence, it would be:

_____

_____

A belief about parenting I want to release is:

_____

_____

A belief I want to embrace instead is:

_____

_____

One habit I will start today to shift my parenting approach is:

_____

_____

When I feel triggered by my child, I will remind myself:

_____

_____

A new phrase or affirmation I want to model in my home is:

_____

_____

Example: *"All feelings are welcome here." "Mistakes are how we learn." "I am a work in progress, and that's okay."*

Exercise: Releasing Unhelpful Parenting Habits

This guided journaling practice aims to help you identify, understand, and let go of parenting patterns that no longer serve you.

Step 1: Identify the Habit

Think of a parenting habit or reaction you often default to that doesn't feel aligned with the kind of parent you want to be.

What is this habit? Example: *Yelling when feeling overwhelmed, over-explaining boundaries, avoiding difficult conversations, dismissing emotions, etc.*

_____

_____

_____

When did you first notice this habit in your parenting?

_____

_____

_____

Where do you think it comes from? Did you see this modeled in your own upbringing? Was it a survival strategy you picked up to manage stress?

_____

_____

_____

Step 2: What is its Impact?

How does this habit make you feel after you react this way? Do you feel guilt, frustration, exhaustion?

_____

_____

_____

How does this habit impact your child? Does it create distance, fear, insecurity, confusion? Or does it reinforce something you don't want to pass down?

_____

_____

_____

What is this habit trying to protect or accomplish? Example: *"I yell because I feel unheard,"* or *"I dismiss emotions because I was taught to suppress mine."*

_____

_____

_____

Step 3: Rewrite the Habit

Imagine yourself responding in a way that aligns with the parent you want to be. What would a healthier reaction look like?

_____

_____

_____

What's one small action you can take next time you notice yourself falling into this habit? Example: *Instead of yelling, I will take a deep breath before responding.*

_____

_____

_____

What mantra or phrase can you use to remind yourself of this change? Example: *"I am learning a new way." "I can pause and choose differently."*

_____

_____

_____

Step 4: Commit to Growth

When this habit shows up, how will you show yourself grace instead of self-judgment?

_____

_____

_____

How will you track your progress and celebrate even small wins?

_____

_____

_____

Who or what can support you in maintaining this change? Example: *A friend, a reminder on your phone, a note on your fridge?*

_____

_____

_____

Final Reflection

Moving toward intentional and conscious parenting is a decision for growth. Rather than getting caught in an endless cycle of blame—where fault is passed from one generation to the next—it's essential to break free from a victim mindset and embrace self-awareness. Evolving as a parent means stepping off autopilot and making deliberate, value-driven choices, even when that requires hard work.

Celebrate yourself for every small step you take toward greater self-awareness, knowing that each act of conscious parenting not only transforms your life but also shapes the lives of your children and future generations. Remember, this journey isn't about erasing your past; it's about understanding it so you can consciously create a nurturing and transformative future. Take your time with each step, and revisit this exercise as often as you need—your continual growth enriches the lives of everyone you cherish.

CHAPTER 3

THE EMOTIONAL MIRROR AND HOW FEELINGS REFLECT OUR GROWTH

If you're a parent, you already sense this truth—and if you're not yet one, here's a spoiler: parenthood can awaken emotional depths you never knew existed. For some, it comes as a shock; for others, it can feel like an invitation to slip into the role of the victim. But for those ready to embrace transformation, this book offers a path to reclaiming your emotional self.

What does this mean? Our children have a unique power to trigger us in ways few other relationships can. These triggers—often unconscious and steeped in past pain—are windows into our childhood wounds. They reveal the unresolved conflicts that continue to shape how we experience love, support, security, and comfort. Whether these early experiences were nurturing or challenging, they become part of our self-perception, influencing our reactions today.

Consider the moment when your toddler tosses food on the floor. In that heated instant, you might react with disproportionate anger, perhaps chastising your child for a perceived lapse in attention or thoughtfulness. This intense response is not merely about spilled food—it's an emotional trigger that echoes the high, often unrealistic standards of perfection imposed on you as a child.

The irony is that once the storm of emotions subsides, you're left dismayed by the person you became in that moment. Deep down, you feel empathy and compassion for your little one, recognizing that their mistake was neither malicious nor intentional. Yet, in the crucible of the moment, those buried wounds surge to the surface, making it nearly impossible to respond with calm and measured care.

The work you're embarking on in this book will guide you toward a different path—one where you can acknowledge these triggers, understand their origins, and ultimately choose a more compassionate, intentional response. It is a journey of healing, one that empowers you to rewrite the script passed down through generations, creating a nurturing and supportive environment for both yourself and your children.

What Are Emotional Triggers?

An emotional trigger can be almost anything—a behavior, a scent, a memory, an event, or even someone's words. These stimuli prompt intense, often negative, reactions within us, regardless of our current activities or state of mind.

Emotional triggers are deeply personal. What sets one person off might barely register for another. In the realm of parenthood, recognizing your unique triggers can be especially challenging. Amid the high stakes of raising children, where anxiety and stress are everyday companions, it's almost expected to overreact—think of that half-hour tantrum in the early hours of the morning.

Yet beyond these shared, often chaotic moments, there lie specific behaviors or situations involving your children that push you to your limit. These are the instances where your reaction feels disproportionately intense, almost as if it belongs to someone else entirely. In these moments, you are likely encountering echoes of your own childhood wounds—the unresolved emotions that have quietly shaped you over the years.

By pinpointing these particular triggers, you open a pathway to understanding your past and the deep-seated experiences that continue to influence your present. This awareness is the first step in transforming your reactions, allowing you to parent with greater calm, compassion, and intentionality.

How our Emotional Triggers Reveal our Inner Wounds

Have you ever noticed that you feel unusually sensitive when you sense your child might be rejecting or ignoring you? Such moments may be more than just fleeting emotions; they can be echoes of past pain—reminders of times in your own childhood when you felt overlooked or abandoned by those who were meant to care for you.

Consider, for example, the parent who becomes excessively controlling when a child shows signs of wanting to make independent choices—even something as simple as choosing an outfit for kindergarten. This need to micromanage often stems from a childhood where a healthy sense of autonomy was absent. For these parents, the freedom to explore is tangled with fear, as they have come to associate independence with potential danger.

Then there are those who become unusually defensive when faced with any hint of criticism from their children. This reaction, too, has its roots in earlier experiences—a time when criticism and judgment were frequent visitors in their young lives. The wounds inflicted by those moments can leave us with an intolerance for any form of perceived disapproval, especially from the very children we are now raising.

These examples illuminate a crucial truth: our emotional triggers are not random. They are windows into our inner world, reflecting deep-seated wounds from our past. By recognizing these triggers, you can begin to understand the origins of your responses and, in turn, nurture a more compassionate and conscious approach to parenting.

Parents with unrealistic expectations for their children's achievements or behavior are not uncommon. Deep down, we all want our children to reach their full potential and live their best lives. However, when our standards become excessively high, we may be, perhaps unconsciously, projecting our own feelings of inadequacy. We begin to expect perfection not because our children deserve it, but because we fear they might not mirror the idealized version of ourselves that we once longed for.

I, too, have faced this challenge—the struggle to regulate my own emotions when my child acts out. I remember a day when my son was overwhelmed by his emotions. As he cried and struggled to express himself, fear and uncertainty took hold of me. In my panic, I expected him to quickly calm down and clearly explain what he felt—a standard that was far from realistic for a child. That unrealistic expectation led me to dismiss his outburst as mere misbehavior, only to realize later that my reaction had escalated the situation and left us both feeling hurt. It was a tough lesson in the importance of meeting him where he is and managing my own emotions with compassion.

It's important to remember that children are still developing; their limbic systems—the very part of the brain that governs emotion, behavior, memory, and motivation—are still maturing, making it natural for them to experience emotions in a raw, unfiltered manner.

This particular emotional trigger often has its roots in our own childhoods—a time when we may have lacked the emotional support necessary to develop healthy regulation skills. When we didn't receive the care and understanding we needed as children, it can be especially challenging to navigate our children's big, turbulent emotions. Our unresolved wounds resurface, causing our own emotions to flare just as fiercely as those of our little ones.

By acknowledging these patterns and understanding their origins, we take the first steps toward breaking free from them. In doing so, we can learn to respond with empathy and balance, nurturing not only our children's growth but also our own emotional well-being.

Reacting vs. Responding: A Self-Regulation Framework

The journey from reacting to responding begins with a single, transformative step: self-awareness. It starts by identifying your emotional triggers and pausing—just for a moment—when they surface. This practice may feel uncomfortable at first, but it holds the key to revealing the underlying patterns that shape your reactions.

When you feel a trigger arise, try to find a few moments of solitude. Close your eyes, take a deep, mindful breath, and allow yourself to fully experience the intensity and discomfort that arise within. Notice the sensations in your body, the unique emotions that swell inside, and the overall weight of these feelings. Rather than trying to analyze, fix, or dismiss them, simply observe them with gentle curiosity. In many cases, as you give these emotions space to exist without interference, they begin to soften and gradually fade away.

To deepen your self-awareness, keep a "Trigger Journal" for one week. Each time you notice a strong emotional reaction to your child, record the following:

- **The Behavior That Triggered You:** For example, "My child refused to listen to me."

- **Your Immediate Reaction:** Perhaps, "I felt ignored and snapped at them."

- **The Underlying Emotion:** Such as, "I felt rejected and disrespected."

- **A Possible Childhood Connection:** Maybe, "I often felt unheard as a child."

At the end of the week, review your notes. Look for patterns and recurring themes. This reflective process can unveil the hidden roots of your triggers, connecting past experiences with your present emotional landscape.

With these insights in hand, begin to explore ways to respond thoughtfully instead of impulsively. Notice how empowering it is to reclaim your choices, to decide your actions rather than letting raw emotions dictate your behavior. Over time, this practice will help you transition from mere reactivity into a space of conscious, nurturing response—one that not only enriches your relationship with your child but also fosters your own inner resilience and peace.

Practical Exercises to Improve Emotional Awareness

When we first embarked on our journey of motherhood, many of us had no inkling that it would awaken emotions we never knew existed. There are moments filled with profound fulfillment and heart-opening joy, and then there are those unexpected instances that leave us feeling raw and overwhelmed. Remember: our children do not create these feelings—they simply reveal them. They hold up a mirror, reflecting back the wounds, unmet needs, and long-held patterns that have traveled with us since childhood.

Embrace this vulnerability. See it as an opportunity to break free from old cycles. Allow yourself to sit with these emotions rather than push them away. In that space of acceptance, understanding begins to emerge, and with that understanding comes the power to choose a different path.

Here are a few exercises to deepen your emotional awareness on your parenting journey. Take a moment to reflect in the space between chaos and calm, and let these practices gently guide you toward greater self-understanding and nurturing transformation.

Remember, every moment of vulnerability is an opportunity for growth. As you nurture your emotional awareness, you not only transform your own inner landscape but also create a more loving and resilient environment for your children. Embrace these exercises as a sacred part of your journey—a journey toward understanding, healing, and authentic, mindful parenting.

Step 1: The Pause Between Feeling and Reaction

Think about the last time you felt overwhelmed, frustrated, or hurt by your child's behavior.

What was the exact moment you felt the shift from calm to reactive?

_____

_____

_____

_____

If you could slow time down, what would you tell yourself in that space between the trigger and your reaction?

_____

_____

_____

_____

What did your body feel like in that moment? Where did the tension settle?

_____

_____

_____

_____

Imagine an alternate version of that moment where you were able to pause. What would that have looked like? How would it have changed the energy of the moment?

_____

_____

_____

_____

You don't need to judge yourself for how you reacted. Just notice. The more you notice, the more power you have to choose differently next time.

Step 2: Listening to the Body's Cues

What is your body telling you about your emotions before your mind even registers them?

Think of a time when you felt irritated, hurt, or rejected in a parenting moment. Where did you feel it in your body first?

_____

_____

_____

_____

Did your chest tighten? Did your stomach drop? Did your jaw clench?

_____

_____

_____

_____

If you had paused and paid attention to those sensations, what would they have told you?

_____

_____

_____

_____

Imagine if, instead of reacting outwardly, you took a deep breath and softened into that feeling. How might that shift your response?

_____

_____

_____

_____

The body speaks before the mind catches up. The more you attune to its signals, the more choices you have regarding how you respond.

Step 3: Tracing the Trigger Back to Its Source

What moments with your child bring up emotions that feel bigger than the situation itself?

What specific behaviors from your child make you feel particularly reactive or out of control?

_____

_____

_____

_____

If you had to guess, where did this reaction start for you? Did someone in your own childhood make you feel this way?

_____

_____

_____

_____

If your younger self could see you now, what would they need to hear in this moment?

_____

_____

_____

_____

How can you give yourself now what you didn't receive back then?

_____

_____

_____

_____

Triggers are unhealed stories asking to be rewritten. They lose their grip on you once you see them for what they are.

Step 4: Changing the Story You Tell Yourself

Notice the thoughts that arise when parenting feels hard.
When your child resists you, what story do you tell yourself? *(They never listen to me. I'm failing. I can't do this.)*

_____

_____

_____

_____

What happens when you challenge that thought? What else could be true? *(They are learning. This moment does not define me. I am growing through this.)*

_____

_____

_____

_____

If you spoke to yourself the way you talk to your child when they struggle, how would that sound?

_____

_____

_____

_____

What would it feel like to respond to yourself with the same patience you want to show them?

_____

_____

_____

_____

You are not just parenting your child. You are re-parenting yourself.

Step 5: Looking at Yourself with the Same Compassion You Give Your Child

Imagine your child is grown and reflecting on their childhood. What do you hope they remember most about you?

_____

_____

_____

_____

If they saw you in your hardest parenting moments, what do you hope they understand?

_____

_____

_____

_____

Can you allow yourself to see what they would see? That you are trying. That you are learning. That you are showing up the best way you know how.

_____

_____

_____

_____

Self-awareness is not aimed at fixing yourself. It's to see yourself clearly and choose to meet yourself with love anyway.

Final Reflection

Parenting is one of life's most unique and transformative journeys, revealing parts of ourselves we never knew existed. Our children have a remarkable way of unearthing deep-seated emotions, stirring unresolved wounds from our own past, and sometimes provoking reactions that catch us off guard. These unexpected emotional triggers—often subtle and rooted in our childhood—offer us a mirror into our own history, influencing the way we respond to our little ones.

Recognizing these patterns is the first courageous step toward meaningful change. It allows us to break free from cycles of reactivity, opening up space for patience, understanding, and compassion in our daily interactions. Embrace this journey of self-discovery and healing, knowing that with every mindful moment, you are nurturing not only your child but also the resilient, compassionate parent within you.

PART 2

CULTIVATING SELF-AWARENESS

CHAPTER 4:

BUILDING MINDFUL HABITS FOR EVERYDAY AWARENESS

Mindfulness is often dismissed as just another buzzword, but for a mother striving to be her best self while nurturing her children, it takes on a profound significance. At its core, mindfulness is about fully engaging with the present moment—because truly, the present is everything.

Yet, embracing mindfulness means inviting ourselves to be in direct contact with every facet of our experience—our emotions, thoughts, and sensations—whether they are joyful or painful. Our minds, naturally wired to chase pleasure and evade discomfort, must learn to sit with the full spectrum of life. Mindfulness gently recalibrates this instinct, urging us to slow down and welcome everything: the good, the bad, and the ugly. In doing so, it becomes an indispensable tool for cultivating self-awareness, resilience, and compassionate parenting.

The practice of mindfulness is our gateway out of autopilot, allowing us to truly observe the undercurrents behind our actions, decisions, and interactions. Consider it as stepping back to witness the chain of events: a trigger, a thought or emotion, a behavior, and finally a result. Mindfulness invites you to pause and observe this sequence without judgment—without immediately trying to analyze or fix anything.

Every parent encounters triggers, and the ripple effects of our reactions impact not only us but our children as well. Imagine this common scenario: a child throws a tantrum (trigger) → you feel overwhelmed and think, "I can't deal with this" (emotion/thought) → you raise your voice (behavior) → the child eventually calms down, but you're left feeling like a bad mother (result). By cultivating mindful habits, you can break this cycle, emerging with a renewed sense of self-empowerment and awareness.

Mindfulness, like any skill, doesn't come naturally—it must be practiced, much like cooking or gardening. Over time, as you integrate these mindful practices into your daily life, they will become second nature, transforming your approach to parenting and nurturing a more compassionate, present, and empowered version of yourself.

In the whirlwind of parenthood, finding a moment of peace can feel nearly impossible. Amid the noise, endless to-do lists, and an emotional rollercoaster, every second seems claimed by the needs of your child. Yet, even in the midst of chaos, you can carve out brief, intentional moments of self-awareness for yourself.

The beauty of these techniques is that they don't require a quiet meditation room, a long bath, or elaborate rituals. They're simple one-minute resets designed to ground you and pull you out of overwhelm. So when you feel the pressure mounting, take that minute—breathe, observe, and reconnect with yourself. In these small pockets of calm, you'll find the strength and clarity to keep nurturing both your child and your own well-being.

1. The 5-4-3-2-1 Grounding Method

When your mind is racing, and stress is building, bring yourself back to the present with this simple technique.

Take a deep breath and name:

- 5 things you can see (*your child's toy, the sky, your hands, a book, the floor beneath you*)

- 4 things you can touch *(the fabric of your shirt, the smoothness of a cup, your hair, the warmth of your skin)*
- 3 things you can hear *(distant laughter, the hum of the refrigerator, your own breathing)*
- 2 things you can smell *(coffee, laundry detergent, your child's shampoo)*
- 1 thing you can taste *(sip of tea, mint from your toothpaste, the air itself)*

2. *The "One Conscious Breath" Reset*

When you feel overstimulated, overwhelmed, or on the edge of frustration, use this simple breath technique to reset your nervous system.

- Inhale slowly through your nose for four seconds.
- Hold your breath gently for two seconds.
- Exhale completely through your mouth for six seconds.
- Pause for two seconds before your next breath.

Try this just once. Notice if you feel even 1% more present, that's all you need.

3. *The "Hand on Heart" Self-Compassion Check-In*

For the moments when you feel like you're failing, losing patience, or doubting yourself as a mom.

1. Place your hand on your heart.

2. Close your eyes, take a deep breath, and say to yourself:
   - *"This is a hard moment."*
   - *"Other moms feel this way, too."*
   - *"I am doing the best I can right now."*

3. Breathe into that truth. Let yourself soften.

4. *"Mindful Sips" – Using Everyday Moments as a Reset*

If sitting down to meditate feels impossible, use daily routines as a mindfulness anchor instead.

- Drinking coffee or tea? Notice the warmth of the cup, the aroma, the taste. Let yourself be fully present for one sip.
- Washing your hands? Feel the temperature of the water, the sensation of your skin.
- Rocking your child to sleep? Instead of thinking about what's next, tune into their breath, their warmth, their presence.

5. *The "Three Deep Breaths Before..." Rule*

Before reacting, before rushing, before speaking—pause for three deep breaths.

- Before you correct your child → Take three breaths.
- Before you move on to the next task → Take three breaths.
- Before you pick up your phone → Take three breaths.

6. *The "One Task at a Time" Rule*

Multitasking might feel productive, but most of the time, it leaves you feeling scattered and exhausted. Instead, try focusing on one thing at a time, even for just a few minutes.

- When playing with your child → Put the phone away, even for five minutes, and truly engage.
- When eating → Slow down and taste each bite instead of rushing through your meal.
- When folding laundry → Feel the textures, notice the warmth, and allow it to be a grounding moment.

7. *Micro-Moments of Gratitude*

Motherhood is full of hard moments... But also tiny, beautiful ones that often go unnoticed. Try making gratitude a habit in the middle of your day.

- When your child laughs → Pause and really soak in the sound.
- When you're holding them → Take a second to appreciate their warmth and presence.
- When the house is quiet → Breathe in the stillness before rushing to the next task.

8. *The "Five-Second Hug" Reset*

Physical connection is one of the easiest ways to reset your nervous system.

- When you feel disconnected, stop and give your child a full, deep five-second hug.
- If they're too busy, try it with your partner, a friend, or even yourself—place your hands over your heart and take a deep breath.

9. *The "End-of-Day Let-Go" Ritual*

At the end of the day, instead of replaying what went wrong, practice letting go.

Before bed, ask yourself:

- What is one thing I did well today as a mom? (*Even if it was just showing up.*)
- What is one thing I can forgive myself for? (*Because perfection isn't the goal—presence is.*)
- What is one thing I'm grateful for today? (*No matter how small.*)

10. *The "Breathing with Your Child" Moment*

When your child is upset, instead of immediately trying to fix the situation, try this:

1. Get down to their level.

2. Take a deep breath. (*Let them see and hear you do it.*)

3. Say: "Let's take a deep breath together."

4. Pause before reacting.

Journal Prompts for Mindful Motherhood

What does being present feel like in my body? How do I know when I am truly in the moment?

_____

_____

_____

_____

_____

When was the last time I slowed down and really soaked in a simple moment? What was happening?

_____

_____

_____

_____

_____

What small daily ritual can I turn into a mindful practice? How can I bring more intention into my routine?

_____

_____

_____

_____

_____

How does my body react when I feel overwhelmed or rushed? What can I do in those moments to bring myself back to my center?

_____

_____

_____

_____

_____

What are three things in my life right now that I am deeply grateful for, even if they are small?

_____

_____

_____

_____

_____

How do I usually start my mornings? What is one small shift I can make to begin my day with more awareness?

_____

_____

_____

_____

_____

What does self-compassion look like for me? How can I be gentler with myself in moments of stress or exhaustion?

_____

_____

_____

_____

_____

What is something I do every day that I rarely pay attention to? What would it feel like to do it slowly and mindfully?

_____

_____

_____

_____

_____

When my child is struggling or having big emotions, how do I usually respond? How would I like to respond?

_____

_____

_____

_____

_____

If I paused for just one deep breath before reacting to a challenge, how might that change the outcome?

_____

_____

_____

_____

_____

How do I feel when I let myself fully engage with my child, without distraction or multitasking?

_____

_____

_____

_____

_____

What are some simple ways I can bring more joy and presence into my everyday life?

_____

_____

_____

_____

_____

If I could speak to myself the way I speak to my child when they need comfort, what would I say?

_____

_____

_____

_____

_____

What is one habit or thought pattern that keeps me from being fully present? How can I gently shift it?

_____

_____

_____

_____

_____

If I trusted that I was already doing enough as a mother, how would that change the way I move through my days?

_____

_____

_____

_____

_____

What is one mindful habit I want to commit to, even if just for a few minutes each day?

_____

_____

_____

_____

_____

How can I remind myself to return to the present, even in the busiest moments?

_____

_____

_____

_____

_____

What does mindfulness mean to me, not as a practice, but as a way of being?

_____

_____

_____

_____

_____

Final Thought

A mindful mother is one of the greatest gifts a family can have. It's never about perfection, it's about presence. In the midst of the chaos, when emotions run high and triggers take over, mindfulness gives you the power to pause, observe, and respond with intention rather than react on autopilot. It's a practiced skill that helps you break cycles of frustration and self-doubt, leaving you with a deeper connection with yourself and your children. What's best about mindfulness is that you can carry it with you everywhere, as it doesn't require a room or physical space, just your presence in the moment.

In these moments of mindfulness, you can reset your emotional wellbeing, while showing your children the importance of resilience and awareness. You can create a home where patience, understanding, and love can flourish.

CHAPTER 5:

BREAKING THE CYCLE: REWRITING
NEGATIVE PATTERNS

G etting caught up in negative patterns in parenting is more
common than we'd like to admit. These cycles can distract us
from the abundant joy that lies at the heart of this journey. If
left unaddressed, they can leave us feeling drained, demotivated, and
utterly trapped. Yet, even in those moments of despair, remember:
with practice and self-awareness, these patterns can be transformed.

Negative repetitive patterns begin with the familiar cycles we've discussed in previous chapters—the habitual responses that seem to lead
us down a road we never intended to travel. Picture a cycle where frustration or anger sparks an impulsive reaction, resulting in an outcome
that leaves you feeling helpless and stuck, as if no matter how hard you
try, nothing changes. And then, just as swiftly, the cycle repeats itself.

These negative patterns are particularly stubborn because they awaken
the deepest, most unconscious wounds within us. As parents, these
triggers not only challenge our emotional well-being but also shake
our confidence in our ability to nurture and guide. The doubt they
cast can steal the joy from the incredible gift of parenthood, leaving us
questioning our effectiveness and our worth.

But here's the truth: every cycle, no matter how entrenched, holds
the potential for change. By embracing self-awareness and gently

challenging these patterns, you can reclaim your power, infuse your interactions with compassion, and rediscover the profound joy of nurturing your child. Every step you take toward breaking free is a testament to your strength as a parent—and as a beautifully resilient human being.

When we feel that our parenting is a constant struggle, every day can become a relentless battle—one that strains our mental health and our connection with our children. We know that these patterns often arise from the stress, exhaustion, and unresolved wounds carried from our own childhoods. Yet, there's another, subtler force at play: the limiting beliefs that quietly take root in our minds, influencing us without our even realizing it.

It's astonishing how much our thoughts shape our reality. The beliefs we hold about ourselves and the world dictate our actions and, at times, prevent us from making the changes we need simply because we doubt our own capability. These are not fleeting thoughts but rigid constructs, molded by societal expectations, cultural norms, family influences, and—most profoundly—our personal experiences. The more painful those experiences were, the more inflexible our beliefs become, making it all the harder to detach from them.

These limiting beliefs seep into every aspect of our lives—affecting our mood, our motivation, and the way we perceive our own potential. For example, if you believe "I am not important enough," you might find it nearly impossible to raise your hand in a meeting or speak up when your voice matters. This belief not only diminishes your sense of self-worth but also holds you back from embracing the fullness of your potential.

By recognizing and challenging these beliefs, you open the door to a more empowered version of yourself—one that can transform your relationship with your children and infuse your daily life with renewed joy and possibility. Embrace the journey of self-discovery and change, knowing that each step you take brings you closer to a more resilient and authentic you.

Growing up, vulnerability was deemed unacceptable; any hint of raw emotion was quickly buried, leaving no room to truly feel or express difficult emotions. In my family, vulnerability and painful emotions were not shared or displayed—an enduring limiting belief that I carried into adulthood. As a mother, I realized I lacked the tools to teach my children how to navigate challenges. Because I didn't know how to process painful emotions myself and found them deeply uncomfortable, I felt compelled to shield my child at all costs, fiercely guarding against anyone who might upset them. Instead of guiding them through hardship, I became a mama bear, challenging anyone who caused my child pain. In my well-intentioned efforts to protect them, I inadvertently prevented them from experiencing and learning from life's inevitable difficulties. It wasn't until I embraced my own emotional journey—acknowledging and working through my suppressed feelings—that I began to connect with my children on a deeper, more compassionate level.

Now, it's time for us to explore these negative, repetitive patterns and reframe them. Are you ready to break free from the cycles that have held you back and step into a more authentic, loving way of parenting?

How to Spot and Reframe Limiting Beliefs

Limiting beliefs lie beneath the surface of our daily lives, silently shaped by past experiences, societal pressures, and childhood wounds. These beliefs influence not only how we respond to stress in unhealthy ways but also how we view ourselves as parents, guiding our reactions during life's most challenging moments with our children.

The good news is that these limiting beliefs can be reframed. This exercise is designed to help you unearth those hidden narratives, challenge them with compassion, and create empowering new stories for your parenting journey. Remember, Mom—you've got this.

Step 1: Spot Your Limiting Beliefs

Limiting beliefs are thoughts that sound like harsh self-judgments, absolute statements, or self-defeating beliefs that pop up when you are struggling with something with your child.

Take a moment to reflect on your most challenging parenting moments.

When you lose your patience, what do you tell yourself afterward?

_____

_____

_____

_____

When your child doesn't listen, what internal story do you create about yourself as a parent?

_____

_____

_____

_____

When you feel overwhelmed, what thoughts keep cycling through your mind?

_____

_____

_____

_____

Journal Prompt

Write down the negative thoughts that arise in your parenting journey. Don't filter them. Let them flow onto the page without judgment.

Examples:

- *"I'm not patient enough."*
- *"I'm failing my child."*
- *"Other moms handle this better than me."*
- *"I'll never be the parent I want to be."*

_____

_____

_____

_____

Step 2: Question the Belief

Once you've identified a limiting belief, gently challenge it. Ask yourself:

Is this belief absolutely true? Would every person agree that this is true about me?

_____

_____

_____

_____

Where did this belief come from? Did someone in my past tell me this? Have I been carrying it for years?

_____

_____

_____

_____

What evidence do I have that contradicts this belief? Have I ever shown patience? Have I ever handled a tough moment well?

_____

_____

_____

_____

What would I say to a friend who felt this way? Would I ever tell them this belief is true? Probably not.

_____

_____

_____

_____

Example:
- Limiting belief: *"I'm not patient enough."*
- Question: *"Have there been moments when I was patient? What would my child say if they saw me trying, even when it's hard?"*
- Contradiction: *"I stayed calm last week when my child had a meltdown. I'm capable of patience, even if it's not perfect."*

Step 3: Reframe with Compassion

Now, take your limiting belief and rewrite it from a place of self-compassion, growth, and truth.

Here's a helpful formula:

- Limiting Belief: *"I'm not _____ enough."*
- Reframed Belief: *"I am learning how to _____, and every day I am growing."*

Examples:

- *"I'm not patient enough"* → *"Patience is a skill, and I am building it each day."*
- *"I'm failing my child"* → *"I am showing up every day, and that is enough."*
- *"Other moms handle this better"* → *"Every parent struggles. My journey is my own, and I'm doing my best."*

Journal Prompt

Rewrite each limiting belief you wrote down in Step 1 with a new, compassionate narrative.

_____

_____

_____

_____

Step 4: Notice the Pattern and Interrupt It

Limiting beliefs thrive in the background. They are triggered by stressful parenting moments, so pay attention to that. The next time you feel yourself slipping into one, try this practice:

- Pause and acknowledge the thought: *"I'm noticing I'm telling myself I'm not patient enough."*
- Name what triggered it: *"This thought came up because my child wasn't listening, and I felt overwhelmed."*
- Reframe on the spot: *"I'm human, and it's okay to feel frustrated. I'm practicing patience every day."*

Step 5: Create Affirmations That Stick

Affirmations sometimes feel like a way to ignore our challenges, but they are not. They remind us of our strength and growth, which is key to those who want to survive parenting.

Write down 3-5 affirmations that counter your most frequent limiting beliefs.

_____

_____

_____

_____

Post them where you'll see them daily: on your fridge, mirror, phone lock screen, or even your child's toy shelf.
Examples:

- *"I am learning and growing every day."*
- *"I am enough, even on hard days."*
- *"My love for my child is bigger than any mistake I make."*
- *"I can always begin again."*

Final Thought

Breaking free from negative parenting patterns starts with recognizing that they do not define us—we are not trapped, no matter how ingrained they feel. These cycles, born from our past wounds and reinforced by limiting beliefs, may cloud our confidence and steal the joy from parenting, but they are breakable. With awareness and intention, we can challenge these beliefs, rewrite the stories we tell ourselves, and choose responses that align with the parent we want to be. The power to change lies in our willingness to see our patterns for what they are—remnants of the past, not rules for the future. As we break these cycles, we not only free ourselves but also create a new legacy of understanding, resilience, and compassion for our children.

CHAPTER 6:

ALIGNING VALUES WITH ACTIONS

In our rapidly changing world, the way we approach parenting has evolved dramatically from what once was considered the norm. Today, we have the freedom to explore and redefine family values in ways that honor our authentic selves, paving the way for richer, more diverse experiences in raising our children.

Previous generations didn't have the opportunity to talk much about family values or values in parenthood as we know them today. They had a system of raising children in place that basically went unquestioned. For many, it was believed that children could only thrive with one type of upbringing: a stay-at-home mother who took care of the domestic chores and a father who went out to work to pay the bills. In time, this changed. It turns out that children can thrive even if they have parents with a different style of raising them than what used to be done.

How is this so?

It all comes down to being aligned with your values. What matters most is staying true to what inspires and defines you, so that you don't lose your identity along the way. Whether you prioritize connection, growth, or creativity in your parenting, maintaining that alignment helps you navigate the challenges of modern life while honoring your authentic self.

What makes this even more exciting is that a growing body of research confirms children can thrive in diverse environments, provided the foundation of parenting is solid. Studies in developmental psychology have demonstrated that the quality of parenting—especially when it is informed by a clear and consistent value system—plays a pivotal role in shaping a child's emotional and social development. When parents are aligned with their values, they create an environment that is not only predictable but also nurturing, where children feel secure enough to explore and grow.

Furthermore, studies have shown that children raised in families where parents actively engage in reflective practices and demonstrate congruence between their words and actions tend to exhibit higher levels of emotional intelligence. This is because such an environment models adaptive coping strategies and a balanced approach to life's challenges. In essence, parental clarity and value alignment do not merely provide a set of guidelines for behavior; they actively contribute to a child's capacity to blossom into their best self—emotionally, cognitively, and socially.

The Value of your Values: So, What Are Values?

Our values are the silent compass that guides us through the journey of motherhood. They are the deeply held beliefs that shape our actions, decisions, and the very way we see the world—connecting our past to our present and lighting the way toward the future we envision for ourselves and our children. For a mother, values are far more than abstract ideals; they are the foundation upon which your unique approach to parenting is built. Whether it's kindness, resilience, honesty, or compassion, these principles echo in the way you nurture your child, make decisions, and navigate life's challenges. They are the touchstones that remind you of who you are at your core, especially in moments when the world feels overwhelming.

To align our actions with our core values is to build a foundation for conscious, compassionate parenting—a legacy that our children will carry forward. Begin by taking a deliberate pause to reflect on the qualities you cherish most. Ask yourself: Is it kindness? Resilience? Curiosity? Write these down. These core values are not mere ideas; they represent the very essence of the parenting vision you hold for your family. When you clearly identify what matters most to you, you lay the groundwork for setting meaningful goals that resonate with your deepest self.

Next, consider your daily interactions with your children. Are your actions echoing the values you've identified? For instance, if empathy is a cornerstone of your parenting, do you model understanding and compassion in every conversation—even during challenging moments? If you value resilience, do you encourage your child to see mistakes as opportunities to learn and grow? By examining these moments, you can begin to bridge the gap between intention and action.

Finally, set small, actionable steps to reinforce this alignment. Perhaps it's dedicating a few minutes each day to mindful reflection or establishing a weekly family ritual that celebrates your shared values. Each small, consistent action builds a bridge between who you aspire to be and how you act every day. In doing so, you not only cultivate a nurturing environment for your children but also empower yourself to lead a life that is both authentic and deeply fulfilling.

Remember, your values are not static—they evolve as you do. Embracing them means honoring your truth and modeling for your children a life of integrity and purpose. In the mosaic of motherhood, your values are the vibrant hues that paint a picture of love, resilience, and hope—a legacy that will echo through generations. Embrace this journey of aligning your values with your actions, knowing that each step brings you closer to the parenting legacy you dream of creating.

Your commitment to living your truth is the most precious gift you can offer your children.

Setting Intentions for Your Values and Staying True to Them

Are you filled with countless decisions, challenges, and moments of joy? Welcome to the world of motherhood! At its core, how we express ourselves as a parent is an expression of our deepest values and beliefs.

But how often do we pause to reflect on those values and set clear intentions for how we want to parent? I'm guessing not that much and it's only natural (we barely have time to sleep!).

This exercise will guide you through the process of uncovering your parenting values, setting meaningful intentions, and staying true to them amidst the beautiful chaos of raising children.

Step 1: Discover Your Core Parenting Values

Reflection Prompt: Imagine your child is grown and reflecting on their childhood. What do you hope they say about the way you parented them?

Action

Write down 5-7 words or phrases that you hope will describe your parenting style. Examples: *Loving, Patient, Honest, Supportive, Fun, Respectful, Encouraging*

_____

_____

_____

_____

Reflect on why each value matters to you. Where did it come from? A positive experience from your own childhood? A value you wish your parents had upheld?

_____

_____

_____

_____

Journal Prompt

Which of these values feels most essential to you? Why?

_____

_____

_____

_____

Are there any values you currently struggle to embody as a parent? What gets in the way?

_____

_____

_____

_____

Step 2: Set Clear Intentions for Your Values

Values become more powerful when paired with clear intentions. Let's turn your values into actionable intentions.

Action

Take each value you listed and complete this sentence: *"I will embody [value] by [specific action]."* Example: *I will embody patience by taking a deep breath before responding when I feel frustrated.*

_____

_____

_____

_____

Journal Prompt

What small daily actions can help me stay connected to my values as a parent?

_____

_____

_____

_____

When do I feel most aligned with my values? What circumstances or practices support this?

_____

_____

_____

_____

Step 3: Visualize Your Parenting Values in Action

Guided Visualization

Close your eyes and take a deep breath. Imagine a challenging parenting moment. Maybe a tantrum, a disagreement, or a stressful day. Visualize yourself responding in a way that aligns with your values. What do you say? How do you feel? How does your child respond?

Journal Prompt

How did it feel to imagine yourself parenting from your values?

_____

_____

_____

_____

What would need to change in your daily life to make this a reality more often?

_____

_____

_____

_____

Step 4: Create a Parenting Values Manifesto

Action

Write a short manifesto that captures your parenting values and intentions. Example: *"As a parent, I commit to leading with love, practicing patience, and encouraging my child to be their authentic self. I will model honesty, set healthy boundaries, and celebrate the small moments of connection."*

_____

_____

_____

_____

Display this manifesto somewhere you will see it daily, on your fridge, in your journal, or as a phone wallpaper.

Journal Prompt

What part of your manifesto resonates most with you? Why?

_____

_____

_____

_____

How can you remind yourself of this manifesto during tough parenting days?

_____

_____

_____

_____

Step 5: Anticipate Challenges and Prepare Responses

Even with the best intentions, parenting challenges will arise. Preparing for them helps you stay grounded.

Action

Write down 3-5 parenting challenges you frequently face (e.g., bedtime struggles, sibling arguments, feeling overwhelmed).

_____

_____

_____

_____

Next to each challenge, write a response that aligns with your values. Example: *Challenge: My child refuses to listen. Response: I will stay calm, express my feelings respectfully, and listen to their perspective.*

_____

_____

_____

_____

Journal Prompt

What challenge tends to pull me away from my values the most? How can I respond differently next time?

_____

_____

_____

_____

Step 6: Daily Check-Ins and Reflection

Action

At the end of each day, ask yourself:

Did my actions align with my parenting values today?

_____

_____

_____

_____

What moments felt most true to my intentions?

_____

_____

_____

_____

What can I change and do differently tomorrow?

_____

_____

_____

_____

Journal Prompt

How do I feel when I parent in alignment with my values?

_____

_____

_____

_____

What support do I need to stay true to my intentions?

_____

_____

_____

_____

Step 7: Celebrate Growth and Adjust Over Time

Parenting is a journey, not a destination. Celebrate your growth and be open to evolving.

Action

Reflect on your parenting journey every few months. What has changed? What values have become stronger? What needs more attention?

_____

_____

_____

_____

Celebrate your wins: big and small. What has worked out well for you?

_____

_____

_____

_____

Journal Prompt

What is one moment I am proud of in my parenting journey?

_____

_____

_____

_____

How have my values shaped my relationship with my child?

_____

_____

_____

_____

Final Reflection

Parenting is not about perfection—it's about presence, intention, and staying true to what matters most. Every day presents new challenges, moments of joy, and opportunities to realign with the values that guide you as a mother. There will be times when exhaustion, frustration, or self-doubt make it tempting to fall back on old habits or external expectations. But in those moments, your values serve as your compass, reminding you of the kind of parent you aspire to be.

The beauty of values-based parenting is that it is not about rigid rules—it is about clarity. When you are clear on what truly matters to you, decision-making becomes easier, stress lessens, and your connection with your child deepens. Trust yourself, lean into your values, and know that every step forward—no matter how small—is a victory in raising a child who feels safe, loved, and inspired to live with authenticity.

PART 3

PRACTICAL SKILLS FOR GROWTH-FOCUSED PARENTING

CHAPTER 7

COMMUNICATING WITH
CONFIDENCE AND COMPASSION

C ommunication is the lifeblood of every relationship, yet when it comes to parenting, it often feels like navigating a Wi-Fi signal—strong in theory, but frustratingly spotty in practice. We strive to share our hearts with our little ones, trying to ensure that both our messages and their needs are heard, but somehow, the words often fall short, especially when it comes to setting boundaries.

How can we set boundaries with respect and clarity, or express ourselves in a way that our children truly understand? This is crucial because the way we communicate lays the foundation for our relationship with our children. It shapes not only how they connect with others but also how they speak to themselves throughout life.

The challenge is compounded by the fact that many of us did not experience compassionate, confident communication in our own childhoods. Without learning to be kind and assertive with ourselves, it's hard to model that same approach for our children. In these moments, we may unwittingly see our children as extensions of ourselves, rather than the unique, authentic beings they truly are.

Yet, every conversation is an opportunity. By striving to communicate with empathy, clarity, and respect, you empower both yourself and your child. In doing so, you break old cycles and foster a relationship built on genuine connection—a gift that will resonate with them for a lifetime.

The first step on this journey is to practice self-awareness. Reflect on how you speak to yourself when you're not feeling well. What words or thoughts make up your inner dialogue? Recognizing and transforming that inner voice is key to transforming the way you communicate with your child.

Next, cultivate a deeper level of listening with your child—a practice that forms the cornerstone of compassionate communication. Go beyond simply hearing their words; pay close attention to their facial expressions, body language, tone of voice, and behavior. This mindful observation requires you to take a deep breath and immerse yourself fully in the present moment.

Consider this: if you're replying to your child while in another room or juggling multiple tasks, the quality of your communication suffers. Half-hearted attention can cause so many subtle signals to be lost in translation. It's understandable—sometimes we're tempted to send a quick text or check our phone when our child is seeking our attention. In those moments, pause. Ask for a brief moment to finish your message, then set your phone aside, giving your child your full, undivided attention.

By modeling this practice of complete presence, you communicate not only your respect for your child's words but also the importance of valuing one another's needs. This simple act of intentional listening can transform interactions, fostering a deeper connection and mutual understanding—a priceless gift for both you and your child.

Effective communication is the cornerstone of healthy relationships. If you're struggling to balance the lines of dialogue with your children, spouse, friends, or colleagues, remember that true progress begins with mastering the art of clear, compassionate conversation.

Without it, finding solutions can feel like trying to solve a puzzle with missing pieces.

Investing in effective communication pays dividends: it reduces misunderstandings, fortifies emotional bonds, and, most importantly, sets a powerful example of healthy interaction for your children. When you model attentive, thoughtful dialogue, you not only transform your own relationships but also empower your little ones to connect with others in meaningful, respectful ways.

The Essentials of Effective Communication

Let's revisit that Wi-Fi network analogy. With our children, just when we think the signal is strong, we sometimes hit a dead zone. "Hello? Are you still there?" echoes in the silence. Some days, our words flow seamlessly, and our child responds with openness and understanding. Other days, interference—distractions, overwhelming emotions, or simple misunderstandings—can make it feel as though you're speaking entirely different languages.

The key to strengthening this connection isn't about repeating yourself or raising your voice; it's about fine-tuning your communication settings to create a bond that is both stronger and more reliable. Effective communication transcends the mere words we speak. It's a harmonious blend of verbal expression, tone, body language, and emotional regulation. By nurturing every facet of this complex dialogue, you foster an environment where both you and your child feel truly heard and understood—a connection that deepens with every mindful conversation.

There are three essential pillars that ensure your connection with your child remains robust and resilient:

1. Clarity: Setting a Strong Signal
Just as a Wi-Fi network thrives on a direct and stable connection, communication with your child flourishes when it's clear, direct, and

respectful. Express your needs with confidence and kindness, reducing misunderstandings and preventing resentment. As Carl Rogers once noted, clarity paves the way for meaningful dialogue. When you relay your message in an age-appropriate manner, your child is better equipped to "receive" and understand it.

2. Active Listening: Strengthening the Connection

Have you ever felt as though your words were caught in a buffering loop when speaking to your child? That's because true communication is a two-way street. Active listening—not just talking—is vital. When you attentively tune in to your child's thoughts and feelings without interrupting or rushing to fix things, you validate their experience and reinforce their emotional security. Feeling truly heard is a fundamental human need, and in doing so, you strengthen the bonds that nurture your relationship.

3. Emotional Regulation: Preventing Network Overload

Just as an overloaded Wi-Fi network slows down, communication falters when emotions run rampant. Staying calm and grounded, even during moments of frustration, keeps conversations productive. Your ability to manage your own emotions not only keeps the dialogue clear but also models effective emotional regulation for your child. In a safe, balanced space, your child learns to express themselves and problem-solve alongside you.

Mastering these three skills—clarity, active listening, and emotional regulation—will not only enhance your communication but also deepen the connection with your child. With confidence and compassion, you can navigate even the most challenging conversations, laying the groundwork for a nurturing and resilient relationship that will support your family for years to come.

Step 1: Expressing Needs Without Guilt

Many mothers find it challenging to ask for help, set boundaries, or express frustration without feeling overwhelmed by guilt. Yet, when we neglect our own needs, resentment builds, leading to emotional exhaustion that can impact both our well-being and our relationships with our children. This is where the transformative power of "I" statements comes into play.

By using "I" statements, you express your emotions and needs without casting blame or burdening yourself with guilt. For example, saying, "I feel overwhelmed when I don't get a moment to rest," focuses on your experience rather than critiquing others. This shift from criticism to personal expression not only helps you be better understood but also fosters a deeper understanding between you and your children.

Embracing this approach allows you to communicate your needs authentically, creating space for a more compassionate dialogue. In doing so, you model for your children the importance of self-care and honest expression—a gift that enriches both your lives and strengthens the bonds of your family.

My "I" Statements:

Here are some common examples. Sound familiar?

Example 1: Encouraging Cooperation
Instead of: *"You never clean up your toys!"*
Try: *"I feel frustrated when the toys are left on the floor because it makes it hard to walk safely. Let's work together to put them away before dinner."*

Example 2: Expressing the Need for Respect
Instead of: *"Stop interrupting me!"*
Try: *"I feel frustrated when I'm talking and get interrupted. It's important to me that we take turns speaking so I can listen to you too."*

These shifts help children understand *why* something matters while keeping the conversation open and constructive.

Think back to your moments of frustration where communication wasn't what you wanted? What are some ways you could reframe your initial response to a more productive "I" statement?

_____

_____

_____

_____

Step 2: Breaking the Guilt Cycle

Guilt often silences a mother's voice, preventing her from advocating for her own needs. Yet, expressing your needs is not an act of neglect—it is a vital practice that ultimately strengthens your relationships. By breaking free from the guilt cycle, you pave the way for healthier, more balanced interactions with your children and your partner. Embracing self-care and honest communication isn't selfish; it's a powerful demonstration of self-respect that radiates love and stability throughout your family.

What are my challenges with hearing words from those I love but not truly engaging? What are a few ideas I can use to overcome these challenges?

_____

_____

_____

_____

What differences do I notice in my communication when I give my full attention, make eye contact, and respond thoughtfully?

_____

_____

_____

_____

When I am hearing some thing's I do not agree with how can I validate my child's emotions and be a more empathetic listener?

_____

_____

_____

_____

Step 3: Creating a Safe Space for Connection

Confident communication isn't solely about the words we speak—it's equally about listening in a way that makes others feel truly valued. When we foster an environment where every voice is heard and respected, we build a safe space for authentic connection.

If you've stumbled in the past or feel you haven't always been the listener you aspire to be, forgive yourself now. Embrace this moment as an opportunity to reframe your approach and commit to becoming a more effective, compassionate listener. By doing so, you not only deepen your relationships with your children and loved ones, but you also nurture a more understanding, harmonious home.

What challenges do I face when I hear words from loved ones without fully engaging? What are a few ideas I can use to overcome these challenges?

_____

_____

_____

_____

What differences do I notice in my communication when I give my full attention, make eye contact, and respond thoughtfully?

_____

_____

_____

_____

When I am hearing something I do not agree with how can I validate my child's emotions and be a more empathetic listener?

_____

_____

_____

_____

Step 4: Practical Listening Strategies for Moms

I know that our schedules rarely allow us the luxury of extended periods for self-improvement. As mothers, we often fly by the seat of our pants, seizing each moment as it comes—and that's perfectly okay. Yet, even in the whirlwind of daily life, the art of reflective listening can empower you to become the superwoman you aspire to be.

Consider these simple strategies to weave mindful listening into your everyday routine:

- **Pause and Reflect:** Even a brief pause before responding can make all the difference. Take a deep breath and allow yourself a moment to truly hear what your child is sharing.
- **Mirror Back:** Reflect their feelings by paraphrasing what you've heard. This not only shows that you are listening but also validates their experience.
- **Minimize Distractions:** When possible, set aside your phone and other distractions. A few minutes of undivided attention can transform your connection.

By incorporating these practical strategies, you nurture an environment where every word and emotion is honored—a small, powerful step toward creating a more connected, compassionate home.

What benefits would I receive from using reflective listening? Example: *If my child says, "I don't want to go to school, you can reply, "It sounds like something about school is bothering you. Can you tell me more?"*

_____

_____

_____

_____

Did you know that you often save time by stopping and giving your full attention to your child than by multitasking? So, when you're busy you may want to consider "slowing down" in order to "move faster."

Step 5: Navigate Conflict with Calm and Clarity

Difficult conversations are inevitable, but they need not spiral into full-blown arguments or emotional shutdowns. In the midst of conflict, you hold the power to remain centered, set clear boundaries, and choose thoughtful responses over impulsive reactions. The key is to stay regulated and approach every challenge with calm and clarity. Here's how you can do it in three simple steps:

1. **Pause and Breathe:** When tension mounts, take a moment to collect yourself. A deep, mindful breath creates space between the stimulus and your response.

2. **Name the Emotion:** Identify and acknowledge the emotion you're experiencing. Whether it's frustration, hurt, or fear, naming it helps you understand and manage it.

3. **Respond, Don't React:** With a clear mind, choose a response that aligns with your values and the nurturing environment you wish to create, rather than falling into old reactive patterns.

By embracing these steps, you transform conflict into an opportunity for growth and connection—empowering both you and your child to navigate challenges with resilience and grace.

How can I collect my thoughts and best intentions when I pause and breathe?

_____

_____

_____

_____

Why is it important to name the emotion of what is bothering me? How does this impact the way I communicate with my children (or spouse and loved ones)?

_____

_____

_____

_____

What is the value in responding over reacting? How does this help me to be a better mother?

_____

_____

_____

_____

Final Reflection

Confident, compassionate communication isn't about saying the perfect thing—it's about showing up with authenticity, self-awareness, and emotional presence. By practicing these strategies, you begin to express your needs without guilt, forging deeper emotional connections with your children, your partner, and everyone around you. In modeling healthy communication, you set the stage for your kids to interact with the world in a more understanding and respectful way.

Yes, there will be moments when it feels high-pressure and challenging, but this is the simplest path toward joyful parenting. When you communicate with clarity and compassion, you create a home environment where every voice is heard, every emotion is valued, and every person feels understood. This, in turn, lays the foundation for lasting, loving relationships that enrich your entire family.

CHAPTER 8

MODELING GROWTH FOR YOUR KIDS

Children don't just listen to our words—they observe our every action. Have you ever tried to persuade your child to eat something you would never touch yourself? You take a bite, your reaction speaks volumes, and they double down on their refusal. Or perhaps you let slip a fleeting "bad word," only to hear it echoed back days later. As difficult as it may be to accept, children learn their essential life skills through observation and imitation.

This means that your personal growth as a mother directly influences your child's ability to build resilience, adapt to challenges, and develop emotional intelligence. When you prioritize self-awareness, emotional regulation, and personal growth, you become a powerful role model. This process—known as observational learning—carries immense weight in nurturing a child's development.

In essence, you must embody the values and behaviors you wish to instill. Your actions, more than your words, shape the attitudes and emotional responses that your child internalizes. Embrace this opportunity to model growth and compassion, for in doing so, you lay the groundwork for a lifetime of strength, adaptability, and heartfelt connection in your child.

There is decades' worth of research that supports just how impressionable children's brains are—especially during their formative years.

Scientifically, this phenomenon is explained by the mirror neuron system: a network of neurons that fires when we observe others. This system plays a pivotal role in shaping a child's emotional and cognitive development. When children see you practicing self-care, handling stress with patience, or facing challenges with a growth mindset, their brains register these behaviors as blueprints for their own actions.

A child who witnesses a parent handling stress with composure is far more likely to develop robust emotional regulation skills early on. They learn the value of staying calm even when chaos surrounds them—because they have seen it work in your example. This ability to observe and internalize healthy emotional responses builds a foundation of resilience that will serve them throughout their lives.

Modeling Growth

Remember, self-awareness begins with you. As a mother or caregiver, your capacity to understand and manage your own emotions sets the stage for your child's emotional intelligence. When you verbalize your thoughts and feelings constructively, you teach your child to do the same. So, the next time you feel the urge to respond hastily or with frustration, try pausing and saying, "I'm feeling overwhelmed right now, so I'm going to take a deep breath before responding." This simple, effective technique not only helps you manage your emotions but also shows your child how to name and navigate their own feelings—a gift that will empower them for a lifetime.

Life is filled with unexpected moments and challenges—an inherent part of the human experience, whether you're a parent or not. The wonderful truth is that within these challenges lie opportunities for growth, both for you and your child. Through navigating difficulties, you cultivate resilience—a quality that, when modeled consistently, becomes a powerful inheritance for your children.

Resilient children grow up watching their parents confront obstacles with perseverance and grace. They learn that mistakes are not something to be feared or shunned, but opportunities to reflect, reframe setbacks, and grow stronger. For example, if your child is struggling with a school project, you might share a personal experience: "I remember when I faced a tough project at work. I took a break, made a plan, and tried again. What's one step you can take now?" This approach not only diffuses self-doubt but also teaches your child that setbacks are merely stepping stones to success.

In these moments, it's crucial to model self-compassion. Let your child see that being kind to oneself during challenging times is not a sign of weakness, but a powerful strategy for moving forward. By embracing and demonstrating resilience, you empower your child to view difficulties as a natural and valuable part of life—a lesson that will serve them well throughout their journey.

A mother who treats herself with kindness teaches her child to do the same—self-compassion is truly contagious. When you model self-kindness, you nurture resilience and help lower anxiety in your children. It's all too easy to be harsh on ourselves; however, instead of berating yourself for a mistake, try saying, "I made a mistake, but I'll fix it and move forward." This gentle self-talk not only reflects a healthy mindset, but it also sets a powerful example for your child.

Remember, nearly every exercise in this book becomes more effective when you embody the behaviors we've discussed. By modeling self-compassion, you lay the groundwork for your child's emotional well-being, proving that kindness starts with you.

Step 1: Self-Awareness & Emotional Regulation

What are three emotions I experience most often in front of my child?

_____

_____

_____

_____

Do I express these emotions in a way I would want my child to imitate?

_____

_____

_____

_____

How can I model healthier emotional regulation when I feel over-whelmed or frustrated?

_____

_____

_____

_____

Step 2: Embrace Challenges as Opportunities

How do I typically respond to mistakes or setbacks?

_____

_____

_____

_____

Do I model a growth mindset, or do I show frustration and self-criticism?

_____

_____

_____

_____

What is one way I can reframe challenges to show my child that learning from mistakes is valuable?

_____

_____

_____

_____

Step 3. The Power of Self-Talk

What messages do I send about self-worth through my words and actions?

_____

_____

_____

_____

Do I speak kindly to myself in front of my child, or do I model negative self-talk?

_____

_____

_____

_____

What is one phrase I can start using to model self-compassion and confidence?

_____

_____

_____

_____

Step 4: Daily Growth in Action

What is one small habit I can adopt this week to model personal growth for my child?

_____

_____

_____

_____

How will I intentionally show resilience, self-awareness, or self-care?

_____

_____

_____

_____

How might my child benefit from seeing me prioritize growth?

_____

_____

_____

_____

Final Reflection

When children witness their mothers striving to become better—not perfect, but better—they internalize the lesson that personal growth is a lifelong journey. By demonstrating emotional regulation, self-awareness, and resilience, you are not only nurturing your own evolution but also gifting your child a clear roadmap for their own success. The most powerful way to teach your child how to grow is to show them what growth looks like in action. Each day, through your commitment to learning, adapting, and embracing challenges, you model a vibrant, authentic path to self-improvement that will inspire your child for a lifetime.

CHAPTER 9

EMPOWERING BOUNDARIES FOR YOU AND YOUR FAMILY

Boundaries are the invisible lines that define where we end and others begin. They protect our emotional energy, shape our sense of self, and establish the structure necessary for healthy relationships. In parenting, boundaries are often misunderstood, leading many mothers to fear that setting limits may come off as unkind or selfish. Yet, when you establish clear, compassionate boundaries, you demonstrate self-respect—a quality that resonates deeply with your children and everyone in your life.

By defining these limits, you create a nurturing framework that supports a stronger parent-child relationship, reduces stress, and fosters overall family harmony. Without healthy boundaries, families can easily fall into imbalance, experiencing burnout, resentment, and emotional exhaustion. Such an environment breeds unintentional frustration toward the entire family unit and, in particular, toward your children. On the flip side, overly rigid boundaries can leave children feeling disconnected or overly controlled.

The key is to find a balanced approach that honors both your need for self-care and your desire for deep connection. Boundaries, when combined with balance, pave the way for a more harmonious, respectful, and joyful home. Embrace this equilibrium, and you'll discover that the structure it provides is not a limitation, but rather a breath of fresh air that elevates your entire family's well-being.

Why Boundaries Matter

A mother without boundaries is like a phone running on 1% battery—struggling to keep going, teetering on the brink of shutdown. When you constantly give without setting limits, exhaustion becomes inevitable. And when you're drained, it's impossible to be at your best for the countless tasks and little ones who depend on you. Dinner doesn't wait just because you haven't established healthy boundaries.

Overextending yourself is a clear sign that your boundaries need reinforcement. When you say yes when you mean no, you chip away at your energy and compromise your ability to show up as the mother you aspire to be. Burnout may initially appear as fleeting moments of fatigue, but over time it erodes your patience, diminishes your joy, and weakens the precious connection you share with your children.

The truth you must know is this: boundaries are not about shutting people out; they're about safeguarding your capacity to be present and engaged in the moments that truly matter. By setting clear, compassionate limits, you protect your well-being and create the space needed to nurture both yourself and your family.

And while this book is geared toward mothers who are seeking to adjust their motherhood in positive ways, the benefits of your journey extend far beyond yourself. Boundaries, for example, serve as a powerful testament to the fact that self-care isn't just for you—it also teaches your children lifelong lessons in emotional health. Remember, our children do not merely listen to what we say; they absorb how we live. When they witness you protecting your time, energy, and emotional well-being, they learn that self-respect is non-negotiable.

By saying "no" when needed, prioritizing rest, and setting limits with kindness, you show your children that healthy relationships are built on the foundation of personal space and self-care. If you want your child to grow up knowing how to advocate for themselves, it begins with you modeling that behavior in everyday life—and there is no better way to set that precedent than by establishing boundaries.

It's understandable to worry that setting boundaries might push your child away or make you seem less accessible. In truth, boundaries create a sense of safety. Children thrive in environments where expectations are clear, and they feel secure knowing that their parent is both emotionally available and self-assured. Without limits, relationships can become chaotic; yet with overly rigid boundaries, they may feel cold and distant. The balance lies in crafting a structure that supports connection while honoring your need for self-care.

Your child needs to understand that while your love is endless, your energy is finite—and that is not a failure, but a powerful lesson in what it means to be human. By modeling healthy boundaries, you empower your child to understand and advocate for their own well-being, setting them on a path toward a balanced, respectful, and emotionally rich life.

Step 1: Identify Your Non-Negotiables

Before setting boundaries, it's crucial to understand what truly matters to you. If you feel overstimulated and exhausted by constant noise, you might set a boundary where you take 15 minutes of quiet time alone each evening before engaging with your family again. Now, it's time for thoughtful and intimate self-evaluation so you can ask yourself: What drains my energy the most?

_____

_____

_____

_____

What situations cause me to feel resentful or overwhelmed?

_____

_____

_____

_____

What do I need more in my life to feel balanced?

_____

_____

_____

_____

Your answers will guide you in setting meaningful boundaries around time, emotional energy, and responsibilities.

Step 2. Communicate Boundaries with Clarity & Confidence

One of the biggest challenges moms face when setting boundaries is fear of disappointing others or facing resistance. However, setting limits does not require justification or apology. The key is clear, calm, and confident communication. Take some time to reframe the following thoughts to ones that are assertive and kind.

You're overbooked and overwhelmed. So, when someone asks you to do an extra thing you don't have time for or care to do, instead of saying, "I will try to fit this in," say:

_____

_____

_____

_____

The day you've had has felt endless and draining. Your child asks you to play, and you struggle with the idea but cannot say no. Instead of agreeing to play, you could say:

_____

_____

_____

_____

This approach keeps communication firm but warm, reducing guilt and reinforcing your boundaries with consistency.

Step 3: Enforce Boundaries with Consistency & Self-Compassion

The real challenge isn't setting boundaries—it's maintaining them. When guilt creeps in, remind yourself why your boundaries matter. Where in my life do I feel the most emotionally drained or overwhelmed?

_____

_____

_____

_____

What specific situations make me feel stretched too thin?

_____

_____

_____

_____

What do I need more (or less) in my daily life to feel more balanced?

_____

_____

_____

_____

How might my stress levels be affecting my interactions with my child?

_____

_____

_____

_____

Step 4: Understanding the Impact of Boundaries on My Child

What is one healthy boundary I wish I had learned as a child?

_____

_____

_____

_____

How did the adults in my life model (or fail to model) boundaries?

_____

_____

_____

_____

How can I teach my child that setting boundaries is not selfish but necessary for well-being?

_____

_____

_____

_____

What's one way I can show my child that saying "no" can be done with kindness?

_____

_____

_____

_____

Step 5: Communicating Boundaries with Confidence

What is one small but meaningful boundary I want to start enforcing?

_____

_____

_____

_____

How can I communicate it in a way that is clear, calm, and confident?

_____

_____

_____

_____

What fears or guilt do I have about setting this boundary?

_____

_____

_____

_____

How can I remind myself that maintaining this boundary benefits both me and my child?

_____

_____

_____

_____

Step 6: Strengthening & Maintaining Boundaries Over Time

What challenges might come up when maintaining my boundaries, and how will I handle them?

_____

_____

_____

_____

How can I stay consistent, even if my child or others push back?

_____

_____

_____

_____

What self-compassionate reminder can I tell myself when I feel guilty for enforcing a boundary?

_____

_____

_____

_____

How can I celebrate small wins in sticking to my boundaries?

_____

_____

_____

_____

These questions help mothers reflect deeply on their own boundary-setting habits while reinforcing the importance of modeling these skills for their children.

Final Reflection

Boundaries are not walls—they are bridges to healthier relationships. When you embrace boundaries with confidence, you empower yourself to prioritize your own well-being while simultaneously teaching your children to advocate for themselves, respect others, and build fulfilling relationships. By setting clear, compassionate limits, you nurture an environment where everyone can thrive—becoming healthier, more present, and deeply connected. Remember, every boundary you establish is a gift to both you and your child, paving the way for a balanced, resilient, and joyful life.

CHAPTER 10

EMBRACING IMPERFECTION IN MOTHERHOOD

For generations, mothers have been burdened with unrealistic expectations—imposed by societal norms, social media, and even our own internalized beliefs. The image of the "perfect mom"—always patient, endlessly nurturing, never overwhelmed—has been woven into our culture, creating an unattainable standard that breeds stress, guilt, and burnout. On the surface, who wouldn't want to be that mom? Yet, the true treasures of motherhood emerge not from flawless moments, but from the beautifully imperfect ones. As the saying goes, failure teaches us more than success ever can.

Here's a newsflash: Children don't need perfect moms. They need present, attuned, and emotionally available moms. Renowned pediatrician and psychoanalyst Dr. Donald Winnicott reminds us that the goal isn't perfection—it's to be a "good enough mother." His research on attachment and emotional development shows that children flourish when their mothers are responsive most of the time, not every single time. Embracing imperfection is not a failure; it's an integral part of healthy parenting.

Instead of chasing perfection, what if you redefined motherhood as a journey of growth, self-compassion, and genuine connection? Celebrate the moments when you learn from mistakes, when you adapt and grow, and when you show your child that love is about being real. In your authenticity, you model resilience, empathy, and the power of embracing life as it is—imperfectly beautiful.

The Hidden Cost of Perfectionism in Motherhood

Perfectionism may appear to be a noble pursuit, yet in truth, it sets an exhausting, unattainable standard that does more harm than good for both you and your children. The desire to "get it right" at all costs often springs from your deep love—a heartfelt drive to provide the best for your child, shield them from struggles, and prove to yourself that you're succeeding in motherhood. But in this relentless pursuit, something truly precious is lost: presence. And presence, dear mom, will always triumph over perfection.

When you fixate on perfection, stress and anxiety become constant companions. The weight of unrealistic expectations transforms everyday moments into high-pressure tasks. Every meal must be a masterpiece of nutrition and beauty; every bedtime, a serene and magical ritual; every interaction, an unblemished display of thoughtfulness and patience. Yet, life—and motherhood—is inherently messy. It's a jumble of scattered Legos, spilled milk, unexpected tantrums in the grocery store, and those inevitable moments when exhaustion overpowers even your best intentions. And yes, there are those days when you literally step on a Lego and become its unsuspecting victim.

None of these moments define your success as a mother. They are simply the vibrant, imperfect pieces that make up the beautiful mosaic of motherhood. Embrace the mess, cherish the imperfections, and know that being present in the moment is far more valuable than chasing an elusive ideal of perfection.

Beyond its toll on your own well-being, perfectionism casts a long shadow over your emotional connection with your child. When every moment is spent striving to do everything "right," there's little room left for simply being with your little one. A mother consumed with creating picture-perfect school lunches, maintaining an immaculate home, or orchestrating Pinterest-worthy birthday parties may overlook the quiet, intimate moments her child truly craves—those gentle times spent together on the couch, laughing over a silly joke, or sharing heartfelt worries.

Children won't remember a flawless routine; they'll remember how they felt in your presence. What they need most isn't a perfect mother, but one who is present, emotionally available, and authentically connected. Moreover, perfectionism sends a dangerous message: it teaches children that they, too, must measure up to impossible standards. When you're constantly critical of your own mistakes—pushing past exhaustion or treating rest and imperfection as shortcomings—you inadvertently model a harsh inner dialogue. Your child absorbs this message, learning to view mistakes as failures rather than opportunities to grow, and may come to tie self-worth more to achievement than to their true self.

The antidote to this cycle is both simple and profound: embrace imperfection. Accept that some days, the house will be messy, the to-do list will remain unfinished, and bedtime might be a battle. Understand that a store-bought birthday cake will never diminish your child's joy, but a stressed-out, overextended mother might. The moment you release the need to be perfect is the moment you create space for joy, authentic connection, and the freedom to simply be. Embrace your imperfections, and in doing so, you gift your child a life enriched by genuine love and presence.

Step 1: Shift Your Mindset to Progress Over Perfection

Perfection isn't the goal—connection is. Instead of measuring your success by how flawlessly you executed your day, reflect on whether you showed up in a way that aligns with your values. Progress matters more than perfection, and the small, intentional moments you share with your child will have the greatest impact.

Write about a moment today where you connected with your child in a meaningful way, even if the day felt chaotic.

_____

_____

_____

_____

Reflect on a recent moment when you were hard on yourself. How could you reframe that experience with self-compassion?

_____

_____

_____

_____

Finish this sentence: I did my best today by…

_____

_____

_____

_____

Step 2: Embrace the Power of Repair

No parent responds perfectly in every moment. What truly matters is not avoiding mistakes but how you handle them when they happen. Repairing a difficult moment—whether it's an apology, a hug, or an honest conversation—teaches your child that relationships aren't about perfection but about a bit of mercy, love, and compassion. And don't forget growth and understanding too!

Think about a recent time when you lost your patience or reacted in a way you didn't love. How did you handle it afterward?

_____

_____

_____

_____

Write a short note to your child (even if you don't give it to them) apologizing and affirming your love.

How do you want your child to handle their own mistakes? How can you model that behavior for them?

_____

_____

_____

_____

Step 3: Set Realistic Expectations & Prioritize What Truly Matters

Mothers often feel pressure to do it all, but what children need most is not a perfectly managed home—it's an emotionally present parent. The small, daily moments of love and connection outweigh grand gestures.

List three things you feel pressure to "get right" as a mom. Now, cross out the ones that won't truly matter five years from now.

_____

_____

_____

_____

Describe a moment when you were fully present with your child—no distractions, no pressure, just connection. How did it feel?

_____

_____

_____

_____

If you could only focus on three things in your relationship with your child, what would they be?

_____

_____

_____

_____

Final Reflection

If motherhood is about getting everything right, I've definitely gotten it all wrong. Mothers are human, not superheroes, and our true power lies in our authenticity. Life is not about achieving perfection on the first try; it's about showing up each day with love, learning from our mistakes, and embracing a little grace along the way. Each small, intentional act of presence is a celebration of what you can achieve. You don't have to be a perfect mom. All you need to be is a present one.

CHAPTER 11

BUILDING YOUR SUPPORT SYSTEM

Have you ever heard the lyrics, "I get by with a little help from my friends"? Chances are, you've even hummed that tune in your head. Now, it's time to put that song into action. Motherhood, though deeply rewarding, can also feel overwhelming and isolating. Many moms carry the weight of caregiving, household management, and emotional labor alone, often believing they must "do it all" because every other mother appears to be managing effortlessly. But that is not only impossible—it's simply untrue.

Mothers need strong social connections just as much as anyone else. These bonds improve mental health, build resilience, and enhance overall well-being. Building a support system isn't a luxury—it's a necessity. Seeking help, leaning on friends, and creating a community of support doesn't signify failure; it signifies humanity. Whether it's a trusted friend to share your frustrations, a fellow mom who understands the chaos of toddler meltdowns, or a family member who can step in when you need a break, these connections provide the emotional and practical support that make motherhood sustainable.

No one thrives in isolation. By embracing the give-and-take of community, you not only nurture yourself but also model for your children the importance of building strong, healthy relationships throughout life. Remember, reaching out for help is a sign of strength, not weakness—and it's one of the most caring things you can do for both yourself and your family.

Why We Need Others

Motherhood is often portrayed as an endless act of giving—pouring love, patience, and boundless energy into your children while managing a household and juggling countless responsibilities. Yet, no one is meant to bear this weight alone. As human beings, we are wired for connection, and the need for support only grows stronger when you become a mother. A robust support system isn't merely a luxury—it's a lifeline that infuses balance, perspective, and emotional well-being into the chaos of daily life.

Have you ever felt that, no matter how much you try, your voice goes unheard, your feelings unvalidated? There is profound relief in simply being understood—a relief too often overlooked. Engaging with trusted friends or mentors provides a crucial outlet for both the frustrations and joys of motherhood. Their compassionate listening assures you that you are not alone in your struggles.

Motherhood brings a flood of emotions, and without a safe space to process them, stress can accumulate to overwhelming levels. Having someone who listens without judgment, who nods knowingly as you share your worries or exhaustion, can truly lighten your mental and emotional load. It offers you the opportunity to feel seen and heard in a role that, at times, may seem invisible. Embrace the connections that sustain you, for they not only enrich your life but also empower you to nurture your family with greater strength and resilience.

Beyond emotional support, a strong network is a wellspring of resilience. When challenges arise—whether it's sleep deprivation, toddler tantrums, or the emotional weight of guiding a teenager—having people to lean on makes all the difference. A reassuring word from a fellow mom who's been there, a shared laugh over coffee, or simply knowing someone is available in moments of overwhelm can shift your entire mindset. True resilience isn't forged by toughing it out alone; it blossoms from the knowledge that you don't have to.

Motherhood is rife with self-doubt. Every decision, big or small, can feel as though it carries the weight of the world, and the fear of getting it "wrong" can be paralyzing. Surrounding yourself with supportive, encouraging relationships not only boosts your confidence but also reminds you that you've got this. Release the desire for perfection and embrace being present in the journey. When you engage in heart-to-heart, mother-to-mother conversations, you affirm that others have faced the same struggles. Normalizing these nuances of the "biggest job on earth" reinforces the truth that there is no one "right" way to do it all.

I'm not suggesting that you need a massive support system—everyone is different in this regard. What matters is that the connection is intentional. Perhaps it's a weekly chat with a trusted friend, joining a local mom's group, or simply making time to nurture relationships that bring comfort and joy. The key is giving yourself permission to seek support, knowing that doing so doesn't make you weak—it makes you stronger.

Finding Your Circle: Who Belongs in Your Support System?

A well-rounded support system isn't just about having people in your life—it's about cultivating relationships that serve different roles, each offering unique benefits. As a mother, surrounding yourself with a mix of mentors, friends, and accountability partners builds a strong foundation for both emotional well-being and personal growth. No single person can meet every need, but together, these connections form a network that helps you navigate the highs and lows of motherhood with greater balance and confidence.

Mentors play a vital role by offering wisdom, guidance, and reassurance. These are the individuals who have walked a similar path before you—seasoned mothers, therapists, parenting coaches, or cherished family members. A mentor provides perspective that helps you move through challenges with ease, gently reminding you that "this too shall pass." Seeking out mentors doesn't have to be formal; you can find them in parenting groups, church communities, professional networks, or even online mom support groups. The key is to connect with someone whose insights resonate with you, who offers encouragement without judgment—someone who advises and comforts, rather than imposing their own solutions, with the aim of bringing out the best in you.

Friendships, especially with fellow mothers, provide invaluable emotional support that makes the journey of motherhood feel less isolating. There is something deeply healing about connecting with someone who truly understands your experience. These bonds remind you that you are not alone and that imperfection is a natural part of the process. While cultivating these friendships requires intentional effort, small gestures—such as regular check-ins, virtual coffee chats, or simply opening up about your struggles—can foster deeply meaningful connections. Remember, support is a two-way street; learning to both offer and accept help is essential in building a nurturing community.

In addition to these cherished friendships, consider incorporating an accountability partner into your support system. This person plays a distinct yet equally vital role by helping you remain committed to personal growth. Whether you're focusing on self-care, implementing a new parenting approach, or pursuing a goal beyond motherhood, having someone who checks in and offers real-time motivation can make all the difference. Unlike a mentor, who provides wisdom from experience, an accountability partner walks alongside you, sharing in the journey of improvement. You might find this partner through a support group, a parenting workshop, or by forming a small circle of moms dedicated to growth. The shared commitment to self-improvement not only makes it easier to stay on track but also strengthens your sense of community. And be clear about what you seek from this accountability—it's an excellent exercise in honing your communication skills and ensuring that the support you receive truly aligns with your needs.

Step 1: Identify Your Needs

What kind of support do I need most—emotional, practical, or mentorship?

_____

_____

_____

_____

Do I need someone to listen, offer advice, or help me stay accountable?

_____

_____

_____

_____

What relationships in my life already provide this, and where are the gaps?

_____

_____

Recognizing your needs allows you to intentionally build connections that fill those gaps.

Step 2: Take Initiative in Connecting with Others

Many moms struggle with reaching out due to fear of rejection or guilt about prioritizing friendships. But deep relationships require intentional effort. Three steps you can take to create these connections is to:

- Join groups with shared interests. Whether it's a local parenting group, book club, or an online community, shared experiences create natural bonds.
- Schedule connection time. Both friendships and mentorships require consistent investment. Set up a recurring call, meet for coffee, or check in through voice messages.
- Be open and vulnerable. Genuine friendships thrive on authenticity, which means you shouldn't be fearful to share your struggles and ask for support.

Step 3: Give and Receive Support

A criterion of a healthy support system is that it is mutual. Short of a therapist, these systems are not just about receiving. Who would want to take on this one-sided relationship when you're busy with your own mom challenges? So always remember to be of service to others as well. This will create a winning scenario for both of you. Do this by:

- Offer help when you can. Small gestures of kindness strengthen relationships and provide you with the added bonus of feeling good about how you are helpful to others.

- Celebrate the wins of those in your circle. This is how you are able to foster positivity and encourage others to continue on in their motherhood journey with an "I can do this" attitude.
- Set boundaries to ensure relationships remain nourishing, not draining. Those relationships which don't elevate you will eventually deflate you.

Step 4: Meeting My Needs

Take a moment to consider your thoughts around seeking support. Do you ever feel like you *should* be able to handle everything on your own? Do you hesitate to reach out because you worry about burdening others? Write down any beliefs or fears that come up when you think about asking for help or prioritizing friendships.

_____

_____

_____

_____

If you've ever thought, *I should be able to do this alone,* remind yourself that strength isn't about doing everything by yourself—it's about knowing when to ask for help. Reflect on a time when receiving support made a difference in your life. How did it feel? How did it impact your ability to show up for yourself and your family? Write down one small way you can start embracing the idea that community makes you stronger, not weaker.

_____

_____

_____

_____

If you often feel *I don't have time to build friendships,* consider how meaningful relationships don't require large time commitments—just intention. Jot down three ways you can make small but valuable connections in your daily life. It could be a five-minute voice note to a friend, sending a text to check in, or making eye contact and having a short, genuine conversation at school drop-off.

_____

_____

_____

_____

If you've ever thought, *I don't know where to start,* challenge yourself to take one action today. Write down one person you'd like to reconnect with or reach out to. How can you take a small but intentional step? Maybe it's sending a simple "Thinking of you" text or suggesting a casual coffee meet-up. Reflect on how small, consistent actions build relationships over time.

_____

_____

_____

_____

By rewriting your internal narrative around support, you'll begin to see that connection isn't something extra—it's something essential. What would your life look like if you allowed yourself to lean on others more? Use this space to explore that possibility.

Final Reflection

Motherhood was never meant to be a solo journey. Building a strong support system—filled with mentors, friends, and accountability partners—provides the emotional encouragement and practical guidance essential for navigating both the joys and challenges of raising a family. When you surround yourself with those who uplift and understand you, motherhood becomes less isolating and infinitely more empowering.

You gain the confidence to prioritize self-care and personal growth, understanding that leaning on others is not a sign of weakness, but an indication that you are truly thriving. By nurturing these meaningful connections, you also model for your children the transformative power of community, showing them that strong, healthy relationships are the foundation of strength, joy, and resilience. Embrace the support that surrounds you, and let it remind you that together, we are always stronger than we could ever be alone.

CONCLUSION

❦

A MOTHER'S LEGACY OF GROWTH & CONNECTION

Mothers embrace a journey that grows ever more intricate with each passing year. In the early days, it is the simple, everyday moments—the gentle smiles, quiet cuddles, and soft words—that make a monumental impact. As your child grows, it becomes the deeper, intentional details—the values you instill, the resilience you model, and the compassion you embody—that profoundly shape their emotional, psychological, and social foundation.

Remember, as a mother, you are not merely guiding your child; you are demonstrating what it means to grow, adapt, and thrive. What is the secret behind this transformative journey? This book breaks it down into essential parts to provide you with a comprehensive vision of what it means to be a well-rounded mother. Out of all the tools at your disposal, the most powerful is self-awareness—the capacity to reflect, learn, and make intentional choices that align with your core values.

Now you are better prepared to:
- Understand who you are
- State your values
- Communicate effectively

- Set boundaries
- Embrace imperfection
- Model emotional resilience

But the most important takeaway is this: your growth benefits not just you, but your entire family.

Child development isn't just a buzzword—it's a transformative journey that extends beyond science and statistics into the realm of personal balance and emotional growth. While research can illuminate the "what" and "why," it's your individual journey that determines how you find equilibrium. This journey isn't solely about your children or you as a mother; it's about cultivating a relationship enriched with love, emotional development, and character-building qualities that will benefit their entire lives. And the most powerful way to instill these qualities is by embodying them yourself. Recognizing that children learn primarily through observation is a game changer—those precious eyes are always watching, absorbing how you manage stress, resolve conflict, and face challenges.

When you prioritize your own growth, you're teaching them resilience to navigate setbacks, emotional intelligence to communicate and regulate feelings, and self-worth that is based on growth and effort rather than perfection. Your commitment to personal development creates a ripple effect—a tsunami of positive transformation that shapes your life, your child's life, and leaves a lasting legacy for generations.

At the heart of everything you've learned is one simple truth: connection is more powerful than perfection. When your child reflects on their upbringing, they won't remember every flawless moment; they'll remember feeling heard, valued, and safe.

By fostering a home where emotions are met with understanding, boundaries are set with love, mistakes are celebrated as learning opportunities, and self-care is embraced as a necessity, you create a thriving family not because everything is perfect, but because love, growth, and connection are at the center of it all.

Final Reflection: Mom, You Are Enough!

As you move forward, remember this: you are already the mother your child needs—and you're nothing short of amazing. Growth isn't about striving to become someone else; it's about evolving into the fullest, most present version of yourself. Every effort you make, no matter how small, creates a ripple effect that shapes your child's future. Embrace your journey with the knowledge that every thoughtful action, every moment of reflection, contributes to raising a generation that is not only resilient but also deeply connected and compassionate human beings.

ABOUT THE AUTHOR

As a licensed clinical mental health counselor trained at Northwestern University, I have devoted my career to unraveling the complexities of developmental trauma and guiding individuals toward resilience and growth. With extensive post-graduate training in mental health and mind-body interventions—and over a decade immersed in both Eastern and Western psychological traditions—I am driven by a deep curiosity about the human condition and a passion for effective healing. Equally committed to the power of secure attachments, I educate parents on the critical stages of child development, empowering them to nurture meaningful bonds that lay the foundation for lifelong emotional well-being.

MOTHER'S CREED

I am a nurturer, a guide, and a beacon of love.

I embrace the ever-evolving journey of motherhood with courage and grace.

I honor every smile, every tear, and every moment of growth, knowing that each one shapes both me and my child.

I commit to living authentically—reflecting, learning, and making intentional choices that align with my deepest values.

I will set clear boundaries and communicate with compassion, recognizing that self-care is essential to my strength and resilience.

I celebrate imperfection, understanding that vulnerability is the gateway to true connection and growth.

I nurture my child not just with words, but through the example of my own journey toward self-awareness and emotional balance.

I recognize that my growth enriches my family and lays the foundation for future generations.

Today and every day, I choose to lead with love, to embrace every challenge as an opportunity, and to honor the sacred bond of motherhood.

www.ingramcontent.com/pod-product-compliance
Lightning Source LLC
Chambersburg PA
CBHW061804120626
46550CB00005B/2133